BEYOND
MEDICAL
SCHOOL

T0150950

BEYOND MEDICAL SCHOOL

SECRETS OF
SUCCESSFUL DOCTORS

GREGORY CORRADINO, MD, MBA

Copyright © 2021 by Gregory Corradino.

All rights reserved. No part of this book may be used or reproduced in any manner whatsoever without prior written consent of the author, except as provided by the United States of America copyright law.

Published by Advantage, Charleston, South Carolina.
Member of Advantage Media Group.

ADVANTAGE is a registered trademark, and the Advantage colophon is a trademark of Advantage Media Group, Inc.

Printed in the United States of America.

10 9 8 7 6 5 4 3 2 1

ISBN: 978-1-64225-144-9
LCCN: 2020921079

Cover design by Carly Blake.
Layout design by Mary Hamilton.

This publication is designed to provide accurate and authoritative information in regard to the subject matter covered. It is sold with the understanding that the publisher is not engaged in rendering legal, accounting, or other professional services. If legal advice or other expert assistance is required, the services of a competent professional person should be sought.

Advantage Media Group is proud to be a part of the Tree Neutral® program. Tree Neutral offsets the number of trees consumed in the production and printing of this book by taking proactive steps such as planting trees in direct proportion to the number of trees used to print books. To learn more about Tree Neutral, please visit www.treeneutral.com.

Advantage Media Group is a publisher of business, self-improvement, and professional development books and online learning. We help entrepreneurs, business leaders, and professionals share their Stories, Passion, and Knowledge to help others Learn & Grow. Do you have a manuscript or book idea that you would like us to consider for publishing? Please visit advantagefamily.com or call 1.866.775.1696.

To all physicians who have trained and sacrificed for others,
so they may find inspiration here and go on to professional success.

CONTENTS

INTRODUCTION

The best way to predict your future is to create it.
—Abraham Lincoln

When the bank called to inform me that the account for my medical practice was overdrawn on our payroll, it was a major turning point for me. A neurosurgeon in practice in Kingsport, Tennessee, for only six years at that time, I quickly realized that basic business skills, and the importance of hiring a reliable accountant, were essential—yet untaught in medical school.

Despite my years at school, not only did I know little about the basics of finance, but I also knew nothing about how to surround myself with the right people. My practice partner and I had many disagreements about how to move forward after this event. We eventually went to the bank, took out a loan, and got that particular financial mess all straightened out, but the news remained a shock, and the tense relationship with my partner as a result of our disagreements was part of what led me to eventually depart from the practice and join a multispecialty group. But beyond knowing that who I worked with was just as important as the work I had been trained to do, I was also faced with the fact that the success of my practice and my ability to do my job were dependent on more than my knowledge of neurosurgery. While I had a trusted office manager who thought things were under control, there was no reserve built into the system, and I was clueless—but shouldn't have been. I learned that I needed to know about finance, but more than that, I really needed to know how to hire the right people and keep tabs on them. What other things had I been naive about, I wondered. What more should I learn?

That's when I got a consultant, and we mapped out what was happening. This led to a lot of conflict with my partner at the time and, eventually, to me leaving to join another practice. After a bit of soul searching and understanding what exactly I was looking for in my personal and professional life, I realized I had different values and goals than my partner, and I chose to get out of that environment.

If only I had known sooner. If only I'd done the introspection long before, I would have never joined that practice to start with. Fresh to the profession, I had originally thought of nothing more than the idea that I'd be joining a reputable, busy practice situated in a great location. It took investing myself in the practice before I'd learn, the hard way, that there was a lot more I could have been looking for and basing these life-altering career decisions on.

The fact is, there was zero discussion during my time in medical school about what kind of practice we residents might have wanted to go into after graduation. No one sat down with us and asked,

"Hey, what are you looking for with your professional career aspirations? What kind of settings do you want to work in?" Instead, I was taught the value of becoming an academic surgeon (that value being: you have the respect of all the other academic surgeons). I also was made to understand that by becoming, alternatively, a community neurosurgeon, the academic people would only look down on you. This is, of course, a generalization, but we residents felt that the academics looked down on the community surgeons— I hope things have changed. I was left to navigate these limited and somewhat negative options on my own.

It's critical that young doctors find the right position sooner rather than later, because so many physicians, as I did, join practices and then leave within a year or two to find a better-suited position. It takes a lot of money and even more energy to leave a practice if you realize it's not right for you. Making the right decision from the start is worthwhile for all involved.

When I joined a practice fresh out of medical school, I was so focused on learning what I needed to learn to perfectly perform surgery, and the specifics of neurosurgery, that I didn't think about anything else. People management, leadership, financial management, billing cycles, coding for proper reimbursement, documentation? Forget about it. Why would those things concern me?

Over the course of my career, I would come to learn exactly why financial and personnel matters, and so much more, are important to consider before leaving residency and venturing out into the big unknown. And I had to go through the trouble of moving to different cities—from Philadelphia to Coatesville, Pennsylvania, to Kingsport, Tennessee—and overdrawing our bank account before I figured this out. (Based in Kingsport since 1992, I began my postresidency career as an employee of a private practice in the Philadelphia suburbs in 1989.)

During my career, I have been involved in a number of practice settings, including solo, single-specialty groups, multispecialty groups, and hospital-affiliated practices. In addition to seeking, via various channels, the practical aspects of the business of medicine, in 2012 I also sought an MBA.

After leaving that ill-fitted practice, I realized that, for me, an MBA was essential. I wanted to learn about the actual management of a practice, of a business. Even though I was in the process of joining another group practice, I still didn't feel like I knew enough about business to really manage myself and my people the way I wanted to. When you have some experience and you start to look at the psychology of your staff, you begin to realize things like who would do well in another role, or who's ill fitted for the one they're in and would maybe work better elsewhere. You're able to predict the future a little more accurately. I credit both experience and the MBA with that realization.

Over the years, I've worked with many types of doctors, and I've seen many come and go through our community when good doctors fail because they couldn't master the nonmedical skills necessary to thrive. Conversely, I've seen doctors with passable medical skills do quite well and, at first, wondered what they were doing differently that enabled them to succeed. Later, I systematically began to study and consider this problem, and that is the genesis of this book.

Beyond Medical School was written for doctors who are just beginning their professional lives so that they can establish the foundations of a successful and rewarding career in medicine. And though it's certainly not critical for every doctor to obtain an MBA, it's been so beneficial to me that I can't help but want to pass this knowledge on as it relates to young doctors. Think of it as me getting the MBA so you don't have to, and now you, too, can benefit from the essential foundations I've discovered through relentlessly sought-out education, not to mention a world of experience.

Architects are taught that a building of any substance must begin with a solid foundation on solid ground. We can think of our medical education as the solid ground and the five concepts of planning, values, communication, surrounding yourself with winners, and practice building as the foundations upon which our personal and career success are laid. Like a building, doctors can erect a substantial structure for their practices and career if the foundation

LIKE A BUILDING, DOCTORS CAN ERECT A SUBSTANTIAL STRUCTURE FOR THEIR PRACTICES AND CAREER IF THE FOUNDATION IS SOLID.

is solid. Likewise, a weak education is a weak foundation capable of weakening the entire structure, perhaps to the point of failure.

So why are these concepts so essential? That's what we'll examine in the chapters to come, but here's a snapshot.

First is the concept of **planning**. There are so many areas of a doctor's life where planning is essential: We can plan our weekly and monthly schedules, our daily and weekend free time, and our vacation or recreational time. Our professional education, clinical skills improvement, and practice growth can and should be planned. Finally, our finances, including savings and investing, can and should be planned on a regular basis. Although we all have learned how to plan to master our subjects in school and training, having a good planning method and revisiting it on a regular basis is essential in order to measure our progress and ensure we are staying on course.

Values form the second aspect of your foundation. Had I done the introspection long before I made sacrifices to build a practice with the wrong partner, I'd have saved myself a lot of time, money, and energy. I realized too late what my values in respect to my practice were, but once I had a grasp on this aspect of my foundation, I was able to apply it to my future choices.

Communication is the next foundation physicians should take into consideration. Beyond our ability to communicate with patients and their families, there are so many reasons for furthering our communication skills in the practice of medicine. Developing a network of respected colleagues, managing our staff, and taking a leadership role in our communities can all enhance our ability to provide excellent patient care.

The fourth foundational principle is **surrounding yourself with winners**, meaning selecting compatible partners and associates, hiring and training your staff, and working with professional advisers throughout your career will serve you well and help you to be the best you can be.

Finally, understanding and implementing a personal **practice-building plan** early in your professional life can make the likelihood of developing your ideal practice much more probable, so we'll cover that as the fifth and final element of your foundation.

These are the core concepts for success that we will discuss here. In the pages ahead, you'll learn why all this and more matter, and, ultimately, that education really is a lifelong responsibility.

CHAPTER I

WHAT WAS AND WHAT MIGHT HAVE BEEN

You can't build a great building on a weak foundation.
—Gordon Hinckley

On a bright July day, twenty-five years ago, two young doctors began their professional careers. They were very much alike, having both gone to good colleges and well-respected medical schools. They had both been accepted and trained in their respective specialties at highly sought-after programs. Like many newly minted physicians, they were full of idealism, energy, and enthusiasm and were ready to take on the world.

Although they began their careers with similar backgrounds, their professional paths couldn't have been more dissimilar.

Our first doctor is Dr. Learned-It-All, who believes he's so smart, that he can't be taught anything—no one else's training or experience counts for anything because his training taught him everything he needed to know.

Dr. Learned-It-All chose his first job almost purely on the basis of a large, guaranteed salary and without regard for the nature of the community he was entering or the key partners with whom he would be working. As the newest member of the group, he felt imposed upon from the start, never felt included in the practice, and almost immediately began to regret his decision. Although he did make a substantial salary, he lasted only a couple of years there and moved on. He relocated to two additional practices in different communities within eight years before finally settling into the community where he remained for the next fifteen years.

Over the course of his career, he chose not to invest his time into business, community organizations, or relationships because he was "too busy" and felt he was doing enough for the community through his medical practice. Although he was a good physician, he never enjoyed the excellent reputation he felt he deserved in the community. He was a passable public speaker but did not relish the experience and was rarely asked to present. He publicly bemoaned the changes in medicine over the course of his career and regularly complained about increased regulations, decreased reimbursement, higher overheads, and less money for himself.

Dr. Learned-It-All grumbled loudly and often to his staff, colleagues, and patients alike about how much he regretted his decision to go into medicine. Twenty-five years into his career, he was still stuck, forced to see whatever problem or patient came his way. He felt he had little control over the course of his day and the broader arc of his life as a doctor. He did not enjoy being in the clinic. His staff was poorly selected, trained, and managed. The office staff turned over rapidly, as their work environment was stressful and they did not feel personal satisfaction in such a negative environment.

His home life, although better than his work life, was not ideal, as his free time was regularly cut short by working long hours. He missed out on time with his wife and kids, and vacations were sporadic and sometimes cut short by problems back home. Although he had a good salary, lived in a big house in a nice part of town, and drove expensive cars, he was heavily in debt. To make matters worse, he had invested poorly and did not have a solid retirement plan in place.

Looking back on his career, he was full of regret. He was not sure he had made the right choice in many situations and frequently wondered where he had gone wrong. He was midcareer and burned out. He and everyone around him knew it: he needed to work to finance his lifestyle, his children's education, and his (distant) retirement. There was no end in sight.

In sharp contrast was his former classmate, Dr. Lifelong-Learner. She sought out mentors and advisers to help her make the best decisions as often as possible—this included investment in courses, seminars, books, and audio programs. She had chosen her practice after residency based on many factors, rather than purely on income, including the mission of the practice and the overall quality of life in that community. She put effort into shaping the practice to her own standards, and it grew steadily and successfully over the years. She enjoyed a rich and rewarding career. Her practice was robust, and she was selective about her patients, generally choosing people who had exactly the type of problem she was trained to treat (and enjoyed treating). She liked coming to work in her office—her staff was loyal, enjoyed their work environment, and looked forward to working with her. She was well respected in her community, where she had practiced since completing her training. On a regular basis, she was asked to give lectures to public as well as professional groups, and she was a popular speaker. She also was involved in a number of community organizations and medical associations.

Her personal life was rewarding as well. She lived with her family in an agreeable section of town and enjoyed her leisure and vacation time regularly. In short, she had made the most of her education and training and was happy with her choices as she looked back on her career. She was at the stage of thinking about retirement and felt she could retire in just a few years with enough finances to enjoy her postworking years.

What had made the difference in these two doctors' lives? Was it their intelligence? Their education? Their training? No to all three. As we saw, they were both intelligent and well educated. They had both gone to good schools and trained at solid programs, where they had excelled. So what was it?

It was something else. Dr. Lifelong-Learner had completed her formal training but realized she did not know it all. In fact, she recognized that her career training had just begun. She realized how important the choices she'd make every day would become years later, and she sought out mentors and advisers. She realized the importance of career planning and understood that it was not all about the money. She focused on finding the right work environment in a community she enjoyed. Once settled, she continued to explore opportunities to learn about the many dimensions of her professional life. She realized that being a successful physician included honing her communication, management, and leadership skills by using any courses, books, and other resources she could find. This included investment in courses, seminars, books, and audio programs. She was actively involved in building her practice from the start of her career and invested time and money in herself and in key relationships within her community and the medical field. Finally, she made sure she planned for and took time off to enjoy her family in her leisure time.

On the other hand, Dr. Learned-It-All was almost the polar opposite throughout his career. He felt his time in college, in medical school, and at his residency had all sufficiently prepared him for his professional life. He never sought out advice or help as he made decisions that would affect his and his family's lives years down the road. He took a high-paying job and began to spend the money he felt he had earned and deserved as soon as it hit the bank. He was smart and well trained and felt that was enough to bring patients to his practice, and they should be grateful he was seeing them. He did not seek counsel from anyone along the way, in part because he felt he knew enough to make solid decisions on his own and in part because he had not cultivated trusting relationships with mentors and friends along the way.

Having learned all he needed to during his training, he begrudgingly attended his specialty meetings as infrequently as possible and did the minimal amount necessary to maintain his license and privileges. He complained about all the changes in medicine and clung to a medical model as he wanted to see it, versus how things actually were. All of these factors combined to make him a rather sour and unpleasant person to be around—at the clinic as well as at home. Both he and his colleagues looked forward to the day he would retire, but he did not anticipate this would be anytime soon due to his poor financial planning and spending habits.

The stories of Dr. Learned-It-All and Dr. Lifelong-Learner are based on the famous *Wall Street Journal* ad "Tale of Two Young Men" that ran from 1975 to 2003 and that sold over $2 billion worth of subscriptions to the *Journal*.[1] While these stories are extreme in both the positive and negative, there's a reason it resonated with so many of the *Journal's* subscribers—it's a dichotomy that, while exaggerated, is still recognizable. I can tell you from my years of work and observations that these model physicians represent the reality I have often seen firsthand. Having worked in several types of clinical settings and hospitals over my career, I have seen doctors who have excellent clinical judgment and skills but poor business judgment and people skills. Their financial and professional success (or lack thereof) and reputations are not consistent with their clinical competence.

THIS BOOK IS OFFERED AS A BLUEPRINT FOR ENSURING THAT YOUR SUCCESS IN YOUR PRACTICE AND IN YOUR LIFE REFLECTS THE GREAT INVESTMENT YOU HAVE MADE IN YOURSELF AND IN YOUR CAREER.

This book is offered as a blueprint for ensuring that your success in your practice and in your life reflects the great investment you have made in yourself and in your career. While technology and medical practices have made innumerable advances over the past one hundred years, the concepts in this book are fairly simple, straightforward, and timeless. I've discovered them over time through much trial and error, but the five foundations found herein are focused on interpersonal relationships and personal habits that are as applicable today as they were generations ago. When applied collectively, these five foundations—planning, values, communication, working with winners, and building a practice—can help change

---

1   Mike Schauer, "$2 Billion Wall St. Journal Letter ('Tale Of Two Young Men')," Swiped.co, accessed June 2020, https://swiped.co/file/wallstreet-letter-conroy/.

the course of your life both in and outside the clinic. The earlier you can start applying these cornerstone principles, the better.

The foundations work hand in hand, each containing elements—such as leadership principles found under the pillar of communication—that can be used in one or more of the other cornerstones. The goal is that you realize that your training shouldn't stop with your residency. You have to work at building a practice, be it your own or the one you work for, that's professionally rewarding to yourself. It's more than the medical aspect of it. You can, as an individual, have a big effect on how these foundations can work for you in and outside the office.

Let's now look a little closer at these foundations and what we'll cover in the pages to come.

PLANNING

Do you want to have a practice and a life by design or by default? You can't simply let things fall into place and expect everything to land perfectly. Be it your financial future, the type of practice you want to develop, or the family lifestyle you wish for, it all takes planning.

To spend years in school and in training only to go on to graduate and leave everything to chance is simply foolish.

In chapter 2, which focuses on this foundation, you'll read about how I wasted precious time, money, and irreplaceable energy on things that weren't meant to be and how you can prevent the same thing from happening to you. I'll also introduce planning applications, which outline how planning principles are applicable in every area of your life. And you'll become acquainted with a strategic planning outline that maps out exactly how to apply the planning principles presented.

VALUES

Identifying and understanding your values will help you make the decisions you need to make so that you're going in the direction that you know is best for you. The key is introspection: ask yourself what you're looking for and continue to do so throughout your career. What you want when you're twenty-five will be vastly different from your goals as a fifty-year-old physician. Your twenties might be for dating, living it up, and absorbing the culture around you as much as you can. But when you get a little bit older, things are going to change. By going through this exercise of introspection, you'll hopefully begin to realize what it is that drives you personally and professionally sooner rather than later, as your life circumstances change. If you do that, then you'll start to make decisions that are always congruent with who you are as an individual.

Maybe you value family life but want to be in a big city—how do you reconcile that? Maybe you don't want to commute, so something has to give. Sitting down and really thinking about some of these things is going to help you as an individual but also as a leader, because you're going to be called upon to make decisions for other people along the way. And you need to be congruent with where you are personally and professionally so you can make decisions that you can live with.

COMMUNICATION

The thing about communication is you may be the smartest person in the world, but if you can't communicate the information in a meaningful way to the people you need to communicate it to, it's all wasted. Being able to understand and read other people and get information across to them in a meaningful way is a valuable, critical skill for physicians to master. Having patients' best interests at heart and being able to communicate that to them are two different things. If you can't connect with patients and make them feel at ease, it's likely they won't return to you, and chances are they won't even consider recommending you.

In reading about this foundation, you'll gain insight into the steps I made to become a better communicator with everyone in my life, including patients, practice partners, employees, and family members. We'll also explore how being a great communicator is key in being a great leader: the two must coexist.

WORKING WITH WINNERS

No one can do this profession on their own. You'll need to turn to everyone, from financial planners and advisers to attorneys and accountants, for assistance along the way. In chapter 8, you'll learn how to acquire and develop a group of these trusted, reliable people who are going to help you navigate issues you would not otherwise have time for. Most importantly, you'll learn that surrounding yourself with winners who help elevate you can have the greatest rewards.

If the people you're working with aren't the kind of people you want to be with, then you have two choices. You can help to train and make them into what you want them to be, which can be done. Or you can do what you can to limit your exposure to them and get other people in there. This goes for your office staff and anyone in your life. You want to be working with people who are going to elevate yourself and your position, so you have to be able to look for those kinds of people and help to bring out those qualities—and that goes back to leadership and communication skills as well.

BUILDING YOUR PRACTICE

And lastly, we have practice building. Building the practice you want is critical. It wasn't immediately obvious to me as to how to build a smooth and successful practice. As I've learned how to do this the hard way (and by the way, I'm still learning), I'd like to make this process easier on you by removing the mystique and instead giving you tangible steps on how to build the best practice possible. This means ensuring that the kind of patients you want to see, the ones who have problems you are great at fixing, will be the ones you get to work with every day. If you specialize in gallbladder surgery, you want patients specifically with gallbladder concerns, or else you could wind up dealing with diseases or complaints that you don't have much interest in. By building the practice of your own design, you can work toward a practice that is professionally and financially rewarding. In this final foundational chapter, you'll learn to do just that.

* * *

If you're having trouble knowing where to begin with these concepts, I suggest using a Venn diagram to look for something in the middle that (1) you're good at, (2) you're passionate about, and (3) that people want (i.e., there is a demand). If you're missing one of those pieces, then you're not going to be happy. It took me longer than I would have liked, but I found the center of my three things and discovered I enjoy the intellectual challenge of figuring out what's wrong with patients, using skills I've developed with my hands to fix the problem, and then having patients come back to me who are happy that I've helped them. They come to the office, give me a hug, and thank me for giving them their lives back. And you can't really put a price on that—it's very rewarding. I'm sure Dr. Lifelong-Learner would agree. And once you've finished this book and can both understand and apply the five foundations of success discussed here, you'll have the foundations of a rewarding career in medicine and will agree too.

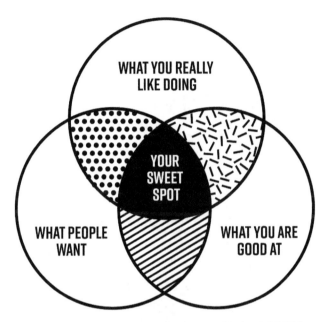

FINDING YOUR PROFESSIONAL "SWEET SPOT"

ACTION STEPS

1. Realize that your life as a professional will need to involve more than what you learned in medical school.

2. Open your eyes to the fact that there is more to physician success than simply practicing medicine.

3. Create your own Venn diagram to see more clearly where you'd like to put these foundations to work.

17

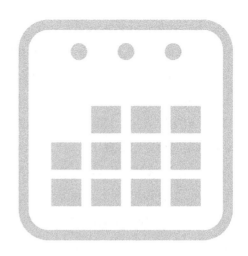

CHAPTER 2

FOUNDATION ONE

Planning

A failure to plan is a plan to fail.
—Ben Franklin

Like many young doctors, I began to think about what I would do following training only during my last year of residency. Up to that point, I had been too focused on learning what I needed to know to become a surgeon to think about the practicalities of actually getting into a practice. But now time was short. What kind of practice was I looking for? Would I concentrate on building a practice based on intracranial work? Spinal surgery? Trauma? What did I need to consider? What kinds of associates did I want to practice with? Where would the practice be located? What kind of salary could I expect to make? Instead of carefully plotting out the answers to these questions, I spent very little time planning this important first step following training.

As my final year moved along (very quickly), I needed to make a decision, and so I hastily chose a practice in the suburbs of Philadelphia. Although I liked my associates and their office staff, this wasn't the best choice for me for a number of reasons, and within a few months, I was looking again. Not realizing how much I needed to plan, I repeated the same mistake and chose poorly a second time, taking a hospital-supported position in a rural area a bit farther from the city.

What was wrong with this position? It was a very small hospital without neurosurgical experience. There was no real plan for building the practice. There was considerable competition from a large nearby university hospital. And the list went on. Once again, I found myself looking elsewhere before I finally settled in the Tennessee community where I have spent most of my career.

Looking back, I spent very little time thinking about these important things prior to completing my training. Had I spent time really considering what I was looking for when I finished my residency, I might have avoided these struggles by choosing wisely and saved a considerable amount of time, money, and emotional stress. Such is the value of hindsight.

I can give you more examples from my own career: lack of business planning in the practice I joined in Philadelphia, financial planning for children's education and retirement, choosing and working with partners and associates over the years. The list goes on and on. It wasn't until just a few years ago that I began to really look at the problems I was facing outside my surgical practice that I began to apply these strategies in a systematic way. In doing so, I feel that I have been able to eliminate much of the emotional stress of decision-making and make more logical choices.

What I've come to realize is that there are specific ways we can make things easier on ourselves professionally, personally, and at our business or practice. From carving out time off to seeking out a financial adviser to giving yourself ample time to prep for the board exam, here are the ways I've found to reduce stress and help things in all areas of life run more smoothly.

> WHAT I'VE COME TO REALIZE IS THAT THERE ARE SPECIFIC WAYS WE CAN MAKE THINGS EASIER ON OURSELVES PROFESSIONALLY, PERSONALLY, AND AT OUR BUSINESS OR PRACTICE.

PROFESSIONALLY

Set Priorities for Learning New Techniques in Your Practice

When you finish your training, you're not really done. Medicine is constantly evolving, and you need to be open to learning new things and accept the fact that you probably don't know everything—no matter how long your residency lasted. Figure out where you stand as far as your knowledge base about the various parts of the specialty that you've chosen. As a neurosurgeon, for example, my training focused very heavily on brain problems, aneurysm, brain tumors, and other structural problems in the brain and didn't really focus very much in residency on spinal problems. When I went into practice, it was obvious that I wasn't quite as good as I needed to be as far as my abilities in that regard. When you're in a practice, there are no longer any opportunities to just go in and learn—you have to go out and make the opportunities. In addition, as a practicing doctor, you have to consider how your interests translate to potential promise. So remember that your training doesn't end as you go into practice—consider what you love doing and what you know you're good at and are most comfortable with, and continue to progress those skills throughout your career.

Prepare for a Board Exam

For neurosurgery, two years of practice is required before sitting for board certification. Although I didn't wait until the month before, I might have reduced my stress level for the oral exam had I started preparation shortly after I entered private practice.

The time between one's training and taking a board exam varies by the specialty, but from day one of your time outside training, you should be asking yourself: Where do my deficiencies lie, and where do I need to focus my education? Is there an area that I know I could understand more? Plan on being studious for that entire period before you have to take your board exam, absorbing whatever knowledge you can so you're better prepared come test time.

Establish Subspecialties for Individuals within a Group

For those entering a group practice, you can't expect everyone to have the same interests and expertise. If everyone specializes in one subject, you're going to find yourself competing with other people within the practice.

If you're looking at practices, you have to ask yourself: What interests do other members of the group have that are going to complement my interests or my area of expertise? For example, in our group we have a doctor who's very knowledgeable about and skilled in the subject of brain tumors, so the other doctors in the group will send him patients with complicated brain tumors. We have another doctor who's really adept in complex spine surgeries, so patients with such cases go to him. But if these two doctors were both doing the same thing and were competing with each other, then it would be a problem; there wouldn't be enough patients to go around. (Either that, or you will have to get very good at growing that area of your practice.)

Improve Processes for Surgical Techniques, or Develop New Approaches

At a certain point after I completed my training, I started to think: What do I really want to do as far as what type of patients I want to see, what type of problems I want to address, and how I could get really good at handling those? So I went and observed some other very highly skilled surgeons in other practices in other cities. I saw an aneurysm surgeon in Switzerland because he had a reputation of being one of the best in the world. I wanted to know what he was doing differently than other people and how I could begin to do things that were similar and emulate his abilities. What I learned is that he had developed a really good system for how he performed surgery. He had everything mapped out very efficiently so that he was concentrating 100 percent of his efforts on the surgery itself, while his staff handled the moving parts around him—that enabled him to do excellent work. Although I no longer do aneurysm surgery, the principles I learned from him regarding developing an efficient, high-performing system have served me well over the years. For a surgeon, especially if you really want to get good at something, you have to practice to the point that you're efficient at it. As you're looking for best practices, seek out people who are doing whatever it is you want to do, and find out what they do and how they're doing it well. Bringing that back to your own practice will elevate your skills and the skills of those around you.

IN BUSINESS

Don't Leave It to Chance: Identify Potential Areas of Growth for the Practice

When it comes to identifying potential areas of growth for the practice, look at your physical capacity for not only yourself but also for the other people within your practice. Ask questions like: What opportunities are there to become more efficient? Maybe try attending to patients with a different problem than you're already specializing in—and ask yourself: Is that something that you could expand into and leverage as a financial advantage for your practice? If so, then figure out how to develop further into that particular area of specialty or subspecialty.

For example, in order for some practices to provide better services for their patients, they may purchase a physical therapy unit and begin to provide those services for their patients. Or another practice may realize it hasn't concentrated on patients who have brain aneurysms and decide to focus on trying to develop those skills and build that part of the practice.

This could work for any specialty, whether it's a medical specialty or surgical specialty. When you, as a new doctor, first go into practice, work on building your own area of expertise. If you don't strategically think about how you're going to build your reputation in a certain area and have patients coming in with the type of problems that you're interested in, then you're leaving it to chance. Although you may luck into creating the practice of your dreams, it isn't likely to happen.

Every Interaction Counts: Establish a Practice Building Plan

After establishing the kind of patients you want to see and the area of expertise you prefer to specialize in, it's time to develop an action plan toward accomplishing those things. Where to start? Why not online? We now have the ability to reach a lot of people with social media, for example, and many professionals turn to blogging.

Not only that, but it's also important to think about how you can use the patients who are already in your practice as referral sources for you. Every interaction with a patient has potential to be a positive interaction—whether it's the initial appointment phone call, the greeting that's to be given when they walk in the door, the nurse who takes them back and takes their vital signs, or the doctor's direct interaction with the patient. If they're scheduling procedures or if they're being discharged, every one of those interactions will be a positive interaction, a negative interaction, or a neutral interaction. Long term, those interactions will determine how your practice grows. As soon as you can, start to view those interactions strategically for the long-term growth of your practice.

Analyze Your Employee Workflow and Benchmarking against Best Practices

Within all practices, the practice flow is the same for every doctor. If the patient comes into the office, they are inputted into the computer program by the receptionist. Their medical history is taken by a doctor or a physician assistant or medical assistant. The doctor then makes a diagnosis and develops a treatment plan. The patient is then sent out into the world with the treatment plan in their hand. Those processes are all the same for any kind of doctor practice, whether it's a surgical or a medical practice. Surgical practices have the additional complication of surgery being involved in some way, shape, or form, but for most medical practices, that's all there is to it.

So how can you best use that process? You can start by developing a good records system that patients are put into, making sure the staff is well trained on using the system, and ensuring that the patients are greeted properly by the staff when they're referred into the practice.

As the leading physician of the practice, you could positively affect the experience of the patients by ensuring that your staff is efficient at what they do, that they greet people in a friendly tone, and that they answer the phone with a smile. Taking the initiative to make sure that happens for everyone who interacts in your practice will go a long way toward having people walk away with a positive experience from seeing you.

Some may feel that's the office manager's responsibility. As for me, I maintain that it comes from the top. Taking responsibility for the experience that your patients have within your practice ultimately falls on you. And the patients' expectation is that you are responsible for this as well.

Decide Whether to Include Ancillary Services in Your Practice

Deciding whether to include an ancillary service in your practice is a financial question. How much is it going to cost to include this service? What is it going to add to your patient experience to have this service? And how is it going to affect the bottom line?

Let's say you're an ophthalmologist, and you want to offer eyeglass services. How much does it cost to build out an optometry facility for your practice? Do you need to hire an optometrist to do the visual exam necessary to do that and optometry technicians? And how is that going to improve your bottom line? You certainly wouldn't want to bring ancillary services into your practice that are going to cost money. So take a look at what you're doing now, what may or may not add to your customer experience, and the long-term benefits to determine what's financially feasible for you when it comes to adding ancillary services to the practice.

PERSONALLY

Financial Planning for You and Your Family

Financial planning for you and your family is important, because when most doctors finish training, they are heavily in debt from the cost of their training. They're starting to finally make reasonable salaries, but they still have to pay off educational debt. When it comes to long-term planning, it's important to find an adviser who understands the particular set of problems that a lot of doctors have—not simply someone who wants to make a buck on churning your investment account.

From day one, determine the best way to reduce your debt and how to begin saving for the future. From retirement planning and health planning to planning for your kids' college education and buying a house, financial planning with a good adviser is really critical.

Health, Wellness, and Fitness Planning

Ironically, doctors' intense focus on work often means they neglect their own health.

What exactly is health? It's not just freedom from disease; it's physical and mental fitness. Plan for personal downtime, which can include regular physical activity. Peak performance as a physician is your patients' expectation, so you need to be as physically and mentally sharp as possible. That means keeping a good diet and getting proper exercise and rest, and maybe speaking with a counselor or a mentor to help you get through a lot of the mental stresses of being a physician.

Therapy isn't just for those who are depressed or burned out. It's really for everyone who wants to operate at a really high level, which, again, is the expectation that our patients have of us. Speaking with a counselor can be preventative, too, of burnout and depression.

There's no question at all that we can't just work 24/7, so make sure you join a practice that gives you adequate time off to recuperate and recharge yourself and get away from the mental and physical stresses of some of the work that we do. Making that a priority for you as a physician is something that you just can't ignore. Eventually, it's going to come back and get you if you neglect your mental and physical health.

One thing that made residency so darn difficult for me was that we dealt with a lot of really sick people, people who one day were perfectly fine and the next day were in the hospital with some terrible head injury, or they were quadriplegic, or they had a brain aneurysm that ruptured, or they had a bad stroke. They were just never going to be the same, and their family was going to have to deal with all these horrible consequences.

In order to do our jobs, we had to put their misery out of our minds, but it really wasn't very easy. Getting burned out from that wasn't difficult to do. Ignoring these personal aspects of being a doctor, especially doctors who are in high-stress specialties like trauma surgery or cardiac surgery, where people are really sick, can be traumatic, whether it's immediately obvious or noticed much later on.

Personally, I've dealt with the stresses of the job for the past thirty years by getting some downtime in the ice hockey rink. Being a Type-A personality, I want to play well—but to do well, I have to stay in shape. I can't let myself get stiff or out of shape, and I can't gain weight, so that's been a really good motivator for me over the last few decades. Having those goals forces me to work out two or three times a week and not overeat or overindulge on a regular basis. I'm not saying I never allow for a nice meal, but it generally isn't every night that I do. So this is what's good for me. I also like to ski, and that involves going to the gym and maintaining some degree of strength training and flexibility so that I can enjoy it.

Maybe you want to run marathons or go scuba diving—having things you enjoy doing as reasons to stay in shape makes it a lot easier to maintain physical fitness.

Recreation and Vacation Planning

Speaking of having something to look forward to, knowing that you have a week at the beach or four days in the mountains to look forward to can take a load off your shoulders. If I know that I'll have three or four days off in the months and weeks ahead to go for a hike or even a day to go to a health spa, it helps maintain my sanity.

Every month I try to sit down and map out a ninety-day plan, so I always have an up-to-date timeline to look at. For example, at Thanksgiving I'm going to be visiting my family, and in the middle of October I have a medical meeting in San Francisco that I'm going to—and mapping all this out gives me something to think about and look forward to. While in California, maybe I'll meet up with a friend of mine who lives out there. Having downtime somewhere special, no matter how little time, is something that should happen regularly—I believe it's necessary in order to maintain mental fitness and clarity.

Maintaining and Improving Your Home

Many people have the experience of going to a nice hotel and looking at surroundings that make them feel relaxed and at ease. It's nice to do that, but it usually costs a lot of money. If you could make your home into a sanctuary that you feel relaxed and at ease in, it can be something that acts as a refuge from the stresses of our lives. That goes for everyone—not just doctors. But we as doctors tend to forget about that, and so the home can become a chaotic environment as well. I know I look forward to coming home and relaxing every day.

One way I've helped make my own home a refuge is by painting there in my own little home studio. There, I have many books about painting, and I can simply put on some music and transport myself to whatever environment I'm painting. For me, that's one area of the home that is sacred. I also have another room that's a library of sorts with a piano I can play—when I'm there it separates me from the rest of the world. Anything creative really is a way to escape and let go of the worries of the day, even if for a few minutes.

* * *

Start thinking more strategically about these aspects of practice building—personal care and finances and so forth—more strategically than just planning out what's going to happen tomorrow. Newer doctors may not consider how long-term versus short-term planning can affect the practice over the years, but if you start to do these little things that make a difference in the long run, it will be much more likely that you'll have a practice that's personally gratifying and professionally rewarding.

As I write this, I'm marveling at the fact that a recent patient came in, referred by someone whose surgery I'd performed a *decade ago*! By contrast, I have a friend who had surgery relatively recently, and she can't recall the name of her surgeon, because he did nothing to make himself memorable to her. Personally, it was rewarding to know I'd planted that seed ten years ago and I'm benefiting from it now. Every interaction that we have with someone has the potential to have a ripple effect years down the road, and by taking care of our business, our professional path, and our personal journey, we can continue to reap the benefits of our strategic planning when we least expect it. That's why we need to think about these interactions that we have with people in a strategic manner—not just a transactional manner. It's not just like they're going to the local mini-mart and buying a pack of gum—many times, there's major surgery involved. The interactions that we have with patients affect them very profoundly for years down the road.

ACTION STEPS

1. Give some consideration to your personal values as they relate to your health, wealth, profession, and relationships.

2. Consider reading and thinking about the concepts related to happiness in the book *Thrive*.

3. Consider how you can turn your home, or a section of your home, into more of a haven.

CHAPTER 3

FOUNDATION ONE

Planning Applications

Effort and courage are not enough without purpose and direction.
—President John F. Kennedy

"**S**trategic planning." Sounds like business jargon to many physicians. We think scientifically, considering problems, their possible causes, and solutions. In contrast, strategic thinking begins with a consideration of your overall mission and a look at possible approaches in addition to developing objectives, short-term goals, and actions and measuring how far you've gotten in order to achieve them. In addition to business planning, strategic planning can be applied to personal finances, such as debt management, savings, high-dollar purchases, and investment strategies. Strategically thinking about how to set our goals and to achieve them can help get to that point. That's not something that many doctors are particularly adept at, hence the reputation that many physicians "enjoy" of being poor financial planners.

As an example, when I was looking for a place to settle after training, I was approached by a recruiter for a position in a small, mid-Atlantic community, as the neurosurgeon who practiced there had gone bankrupt and left the area.

The position paid well, so I was puzzled.

"How did he go bankrupt?" I asked.

"He bought a radio station," was the response. Evidently, he had no clue how to operate the station, and ultimately the venture failed and he was forced to leave.

Due to doctors' reputations of high earnings and little time to focus on financial planning, we make easy targets for unscrupulous "advisers" who are more than willing to help separate us from our money. This is why planning can be so critical for long-term financial success, no matter what our income. Developing more than a basic understanding of investing and financial management should be a priority for all physicians. Too often, doctors leave the business management of their practices and the business of investing in the hands of other individuals, making them vulnerable to bad decisions at best and criminal behavior at worst. Early in my professional life, I found myself working very hard (well over sixty hours a week), and yet my take-home income was dropping. I discussed this with the practice manager. His solution? "Work harder!" Meanwhile, his salary wasn't dropping, and he was going home at five o'clock. Even to my naive ear, that didn't sound right.

So what is strategic planning, and how do you begin? The process can be thought of in a circular fashion, but I will list the steps here in a numbered list. A business would convene a top management team to oversee the process, and the same steps can be done by an individual, the partners, and managers in a private practice or by a family looking to achieve their goals. Here are the steps:

1. Determine your mission, vision, and values
2. Do a SWOT (strengths, weaknesses, opportunities, and threats) analysis
3. Develop objectives and tasks
4. Act
5. Evaluate progress
6. Repeat

Now let's look at the process for strategic planning in a little more detail.

STEP 1: DETERMINE YOUR MISSION, VISION, AND VALUES

In step one, you should determine your mission, values, and vision:

- Mission: your reason for being, the things you do to achieve your vision

- Vision: your ideal world view, how everything would function, what you strive for

- Values: your core philosophies, what drives your behavior

When it comes to determining your mission, values, and vision, do the following:

1. Have some introspection to review your whole reason for being, both personally and at your practice.

2. Write those reasons down.

3. Articulate the mission to your staff or family.

4. Let the mission become how you live in your everyday life.

At one point in my practice, I realized everyone was there for a different reason—I needed to get everyone on the same page. But first I had to determine the main reason that the business existed. What are we doing at this office? Why are we in business? I couldn't assume everyone knew what my values were or what my mission of delivering neurosurgery was. So I decided to write it down and tell everyone.

For me, it's important to treat patients respectfully, getting them the care that they need as best as we can, even if it doesn't involve me doing the surgery on them. Explaining this specifically to the staff helped tremendously, allowing them to understand that it's about taking our patients, regardless of problem or level of care needed, and trying to get them back to optimum health. How can we do that? We're going to do our best to get as much information as we can to figure out what's wrong, and then we're going to determine what our diagnosis is. Then we give them our best advice for treatment, whether it involves something I can directly help them with or someplace I need to send them to get whatever it is they need. Talking through this helped everyone understand what our mutual big-picture goal should be.

I also had to have the revelation that my values have to align with everyone I'm working with. And I have to treat staff well, operating with the mentality that they could work anywhere, yet they choose to work for me. I've had people working for me for twenty years now because they are in alignment with that vision I put forth and understand it—we're all on the same page. Even though I'm part of a bigger practice now, these people have stayed with me and have been part of my team for many years.

Figure out what *your* big picture is. What's the general mission for your professional practice, the business part of your practice, and your personal life—and how do you manage these things? Ask yourself: What am I going to do over the next month to move me forward? What am I going to do over the next year? What am I going to do in the next five years as I progress through my career in whatever way, shape, or form?

Then the next step, as it would be for your practice, is to assess your current situation.

STEP 2: DO A SWOT ANALYSIS

After determining your values, vision, and mission, it's time to ask yourself how you're going to accomplish that mission. What is your practice's current condition? For example, there are certain types of spinal surgery that I can't do. We don't have the ancillary support to do these things properly, and so I have to limit my practice in that regard. In assessing my condition, I have to say, "This is what I consider

> YOU HAVE TO BE HONEST WHEN ASSESSING YOUR CAPABILITIES.

myself capable of doing; these are the areas where I feel very, very comfortable; these are the areas where it's a little bit less comfortable; and these are the areas where I'm just not at all comfortable."

You have to be honest when assessing your capabilities. As a doctor, this is what we have to do. If you're a chicken restaurant, you're not going to be providing people with spaghetti dinners—that's out of your realm of expertise or ability to produce. Assess your current situation, and get a really clear idea of what you can or can't do.

Assessing your current condition is part of what a SWOT analysis encompasses. SWOT stands for *strengths, weaknesses, opportunities,* and *threats.* These things should all be taken into consideration when you're in the process of strategic planning. This is another step-by-step process, and each step needs attention. Here's how I've handled the process in the past.

Back when I began my own independent practice, I began to assess my strengths by looking at all the things I was capable of doing and determining what things I had enough support for that I could be capable of doing a really good job. For instance, I was not capable of eight-hour surgeries, because I didn't have enough support from other doctors.

From there, I had to sit down and determine the things that I would like to concentrate on doing and the things that I couldn't confidently do. I had to admit my weaknesses.

At that point in my career, I didn't have any experience doing certain types of spinal fusions. I had a lot of experience doing one type, which I added to my list of strengths. I didn't have a lot of experience outside that, which was a weakness. I decided I wanted to be able to perform more than one type of fusion, so I made the decision to get the proper training needed.

This directly relates to the next step of the SWOT analysis— opportunity. Because there were a fair number of patients in my area that required the types of fusion surgeries I couldn't capably handle, I simultaneously discovered a weakness and an opportunity. If I could learn how to turn this weakness into a strength and offer more than one type of fusion, then it could be another addition to my practice that would allow me a little bit broader of a patient base to work with.

The final step in SWOT is determining your threats. I have always believed that I should focus on and prioritize surgeries that I know I am more than capable of doing so that I don't get myself into problems that I can't get out of. The threat of having people leave my office unhappy with their services or develop complications that I would then be responsible for has always been a big concern of mine, especially when I first started. If you're not comfortable doing things—which nobody is because you never really have enough experience—you have to work with other people who can confidently step in and help guide you through anything. I've never been shy about asking for cooperation from other people, and you shouldn't be either.

For me, another obvious threat was my former partners, who, for whatever reason, didn't particularly feel happy about me staying in the area once I left their practice. I had to be aware of that threat and ensure I was always performing at the top of my game, because they would be waiting to capitalize on any mistakes I made if I didn't.

STEP 3: DEVELOP OBJECTIVES AND TASKS

Following the SWOT analysis, it's time to develop objectives and tasks, getting a bit more specific at this point of the process.

The first thing would be to think about your long-term objectives. Secondly, think about what you need to do to achieve the long-term goals. Strategically, think about short-term goals as well and the steps you should take this month, this week, or today in order to achieve them. What are you going to do this month, this week, today to move your process forward? How will you measure your progress and make adjustments, and when will you do those things?

Let's say a doctor finishes their training and they need to pass their board exams. The board exams might be a year or two out for them. Well, you know you can't wait until two weeks before the test to start studying for them. So sometime after you finish your training, you have to wonder, "What are they likely to ask on this test, and where do I fit in as far as my current abilities go? Am I capable of answering the question of any one particular part of this thing? Or is there a part where I'm just not anywhere near where I need to be, and if so, what do I need to do to get there? Let me get started doing that."

STEP 4: ACT

Now it's time to take action.

Let's go back to my intention to be able to offer more than one type of fusion surgery in my practice, which I did not have the ability to do earlier in my career. In order to execute that objective, I first had to find more knowledgeable surgeons who were willing to teach me, and I had to convince them that I was willing to work with them and learn from them. You can't just go to a weekend course and expect you'll be able to confidently absorb all you need to be proficient at a new procedure. The first step was for me to begin that conversation with various people so I could find someone who was a good candidate to act as my mentor.

It's easy to think about something you need to do and want to do but another entirely to actually get it done. Don't hesitate—take action.

STEP 5: EVALUATE PROGRESS

So you've executed the plan—how's it going? This is where you should evaluate the steps you're taking to determine if they're still leading you in the right direction. Should you adjust your thinking or your actions? If so, it's OK. Changing the objective and the strategy can be necessary in order to get the results you want. You don't want to try to force a plan that you know, ultimately, won't work.

Whether it's finance goals or skills-based goals, reassess at a specific time—maybe that's every quarter or every six months—and be prepared to start the process again. In fact, this entire process should be revisited regularly, going through the same analysis, beginning with your mission, vision, and values. Have they changed? What should be adjusted?

You can't just do this once for your practice, for your finances, for your life, and then forget about it. You have to come back and do this on a regular basis. Personally, I do a mini evaluation every month (usually about the first weekend of the month) and then a couple of times a year do a bigger evaluation (usually in June and December), where I think about what happened over the past few months. I ask myself, "Are my finances improving in the way that they should be? How are things going with the practice? My staff? Personally? With my children, my spouse?"

* * *

Remember that, as a doctor, you can get so wound up in the day-to-day aspect of your practice and your life that you don't really take the time to step back and look at the big picture of both your life as well as your practice. Personally, I have found it most beneficial to break it down by looking at my professional life, the business aspects of my practice, and my personal life.

Knowing where you want to be and knowing where you are is really

> KNOWING WHERE YOU WANT TO BE AND KNOWING WHERE YOU ARE IS REALLY THE FIRST STEP IN IMPROVING YOURSELF, ESPECIALLY CONSIDERING THAT AN IMPORTANT ASPECT OF LONG-TERM PROFESSIONAL SUCCESS AND CAREER SATISFACTION FOR DOCTORS IS ALWAYS STRIVING TO BE BETTER.

the first step in improving yourself, especially considering that an important aspect of long-term professional success and career satisfaction for doctors is always striving to be better. Hopefully these steps will help you achieve that success and satisfaction.

I can't stress enough the importance of knowing your personal values and mission and practicing that in your everyday life; we'll discuss that in the next chapter as we discuss the second foundation: values.

ACTION STEPS

1. Understand your personal values, mission statement, and vision statement, which will enable you to make decisions that will work better for you in the long run.

   - Mission: What's your reason for being?

   - Vision: What is your ideal world view?

   - Values: What are your core philosophies?

2. Do a SWOT analysis.

   - What are your strengths?

   - What are your weaknesses?

   - What opportunities are currently before you that you could follow through on?

   - What potential threats concern you most?

3. Establish long-term goals.

   - Set goals for the next three to five years.

4. Establish short-term goals that will help you toward your long-term goals.

   • Set goals for the next six to twelve months.

5. Develop an action plan to move toward these shorter-term goals—monthly, weekly, and daily.

6. Get started now!

CHAPTER 4

FOUNDATION TWO

Values

He that can have patience can have what he will.
—Ben Franklin

I have a friend, Donna, who had gallbladder surgery in a hospital in South Carolina just last year. When I asked her what the surgeon's name was, she couldn't tell me because she didn't remember anything but the doctor's (bad) mannerisms. She described him as too clinical, not very reassuring. He treated their interaction like a transaction, showing no emotion, communicating little to nothing about what to expect after the surgery. She doesn't really even recall him acknowledging her with a hello the morning of the surgery. Now if you ask her the name of the lady who was a huge help to her on the phone with the DMV fifteen years ago, she can tell you that with ease. But the name of the fellow who removed an entire organ from her body fairly recently? Doctor who?

That's sad. When she told me this, I couldn't help but recall all the values I've learned over my career and that I have come to find as essential for every executive physician. With the right combination of qualities, like compassionate communication, honesty, trust, and respect, poor interactions with patients are bound to be a thing of the past.

My experience has taught me that in addition to planning, values need careful consideration before you can operate a business at any level of success. In this chapter, I'll touch on key values for physicians that need attention when it comes to the work space as well as personal values, which are essential in everyday life, both at home and work.

ESSENTIAL VALUES

Honesty	Patience
Trust	Intuition
Compassionate Communication	Inspiration
Confidence	Loyalty
Commitment	Fairness

Attitude	Respect
Creativity	Consistency
Effort	Sacrifice
Faith	Tolerance
Gratitude	Integrity

So how did I go about deciding these most essential values? I researched how high-level people work, what they do, and how they think. What I learned changed me and became important to me, and I think most physicians would benefit from at least thinking about these types of things I discovered in an organized way. Let's start with honesty.

HONESTY

As a physician, you have to be honest with yourself about your abilities, limitations, and skills. It's especially important when things aren't going smoothly because when the dust settles, if you're not honest with yourself, you're never going to be able to assess what might've gone wrong (or right) and how to fix it for the next go-round. For example, if something doesn't go right in surgery, it's important for the surgeon to be honest about what happened and assess what to do in a similar situation in the future, addressing exactly why a problem may or may not have developed. Did we have the right diagnosis?

Did the team function effectively? Were there technical errors? Was I prepared for every possible contingency?

Like many residency programs, we had our "Morbidity and Mortality Conference" on a regular basis. We looked at any patients who didn't have the expected outcome from surgery or conservative management. We had to ask, "What did we do here? Why did we do it?" If things didn't turn out correctly, or if a complication or intraoperative problem developed, we'd have to examine why that happened. If you did something technically wrong or you made the wrong judgment somehow, then you have to be able to really look at yourself and be responsible enough to say, "That was my mistake. I did not make the right decision here, and that's something that I'm going to fix next time." To incrementally improve, we must be willing to look at our judgment, skills, and actions in a dispassionate manner and be willing to take the necessary steps to improve.

TRUST

Particularly in medicine these days, there are a host of low-level tasks that we are expected to fill. They're not high value for physicians; a physician's time is better spent on working to find and implement solutions for their patients. Physician burnout is real and partially stems from having to spend valuable time doing busy work like wading through electronic medical records and doing work better performed by clerks. If you're wasting your time opening mail or filling out forms, it's time to delegate—and that requires having trust in your team. Those jobs, and many more, can be done by others so that you can spend your time doing your highest-value operation.

For surgeons, for example, our highest-value time is assessing patients who may or may not have a surgically correctable problem and making the right surgical decision—not mechanically putting orders into a computer. When you look at business systems, it's well known that if you have something that's going to be done more than once, you should develop a system for it so that it gets done correctly, consistently, and smoothly. The same thing goes for physicians for these types of tasks that *have* to be done but shouldn't require the physician's time. For example, an order has to be actually generated into the computer system for something to happen, but it doesn't really have to be the physician who's physically putting the order in. It's worth it to have trusted employees or physician assistants and to have the ability to trust those individuals who are completing administrative-type tasks so that you can spend your time concentrating on helping patients: that is the highest value of your time.

COMPASSIONATE COMMUNICATION

Communication is one of the highest-value skills that a doctor can learn. Needless to say, in medical school, this was not highly emphasized. (As an aside, I did witness some incredibly bad examples of communication.) Sure, there are doctors who learn to communicate pretty well when they're in school or in training, but many of them are less than gentle when it comes to bedside manners. Many doctors' communication abilities are evident in their reputations, so being able to communicate compassionately and thoroughly is essential in having a career that's fulfilling and successful.

I believe that every single interaction that we as doctors have—whether it's with a patient, a staff member, someone on the telephone, the clinical team, or the receptionist—has the potential to be positive, negative, or neutral. How skilled a surgeon you are doesn't matter much if you're unable to communicate with people in a meaningful way. In fact, those skills are then almost wasted.

Real communication isn't taught in medical school (at least when I was training). Sure, we learned how to take a medical history, but what I'm referring to here is real, honest communication—with yourself, your staff, your patients, their families, and your own family. As I've learned, compassionate communication is something that doctors should take responsibility for if they want to improve in their careers. Whatever the patient walks away with in terms of understanding what's going on with them or what they need to do to help themselves get better or maintain good health hinges on your ability to communicate that information to them. More on that later in the book.

Here's an anecdote: When I was in my medical school ER rotation, there was a bulletin board up near the nurse's station. On it were several "chief complaints" patients stated when they came into the ER. These included the "smilin' mighty Jesus" (spinal meningitis), "VD of the lung" (collapsed lung), and "fireballs in the Eucharist" (fibroids in the uterus). Amusing? Maybe in a morbid way. Now I look at this and think, *This is so bad.* Someone did such a half-hearted, perfunctory job of explaining these peoples' medical problems to them that they thought they had these diagnoses. We *have* to do better! How?

CONFIDENCE

If you don't exhibit confidence in a diagnosis and treatment plan that you've come up with for a patient, they will pick up on that very easily. Patients will not follow through with whatever it is you decided to recommend to them if you're not confident when diagnosing the problem or treatment that you've recommended to them. When that happens, don't expect patients to do what you want them to do and have a good outcome. As a surgeon, if I'm not confident that the treatment or surgery that I've recommended to someone is the right treatment, they're certainly not going to want to do it. Therefore, their outcome probably won't be great.

Practice makes perfect. With every surgery performed, I became better skilled and more and more confident in my skills. As a result, I think I can clearly say to patients, "This is what I would absolutely expect the result of this operation to be for you." As time goes on, I have found that there are better and better outcomes for a lot of my surgeries, and I'm confident, in most cases, that we're going to get the result that I tell people that I expect to get.

COMMITMENT

There are many ways that we, as physicians, must be committed. We have to be committed to the right treatment for our patients. We have to be committed to the right way of treating our staff, and we have to be committed to medicine in general because it requires a fairly significant amount of time and mental commitment to go through medical school and the further relevant training needed to stay educated throughout our careers.

Personally, I am committed to constant development as is evidenced by years of reading and attending workshops that further my skills and character, both personally and professionally. But those kinds of opportunities don't tend to fall into your lap—you must be committed to being better by seeking out ways to accomplish that goal. On a regular basis (and exclusive of the mandated, continuing medical education that we are all required to complete), I ask myself, "What am I lacking? What do I need to learn or improve? Where and when can I make the time to make it happen?"

ATTITUDE

Attitude is critical. When I show up in the office, I really try to greet the staff with a friendly hello and ask how their day is going. It's important to start the day off on the right foot. We spend so much of our waking, functional hours with our staff and associates—why not work to improve their days? And really, when you get right down to it, adding on good days after good days makes for a great career. People who have persistently bad days probably don't have a great time—neither does anyone who works around them.

As the captain of your ship, whether it's in your office, the operating room, or the hospital, the staff looks to you to set the tone for the type of experience that they're going to have when they come to work every day. It's totally up to the doctor to take the helm and set the tone for themselves and for everyone around them, and I think that starts with attitude. That starts with taking good care of yourself too. You must make sure that you get enough sleep and take care of yourself physically, emotionally, and mentally.

CREATIVITY

Everything is not as it's presented in a book. Frequently, things are not quite what you expect, so you have to be able to look at situations and make adjustments as you go that will work for the patient. Just because the book says you have to do this, this, or this, doesn't mean that that's going to be the only way to do it. And it doesn't necessarily mean it's going to be the best way to do it for that particular individual. You have to be able to think on your feet and think creatively.

Being creative about how you approach problems and how you approach people, to me, is a unique quality that the best among us must exhibit. Having both creativity and adaptability are paramount when it comes to problem-solving with quickness.

PATIENCE

There's a time and a place for both creativity as well as patience. Whether it's at home or at the hospital, not everything can go as planned, so you're going to need patience. Sometimes just sitting back and letting things happen is a better approach than trying to force things and ending up with a bad result. At the beginning of my career, I really tried to force things early on rather than patiently waiting and getting a much better result. Sometimes it's very difficult to wait for others to do their jobs, whether it's the nurse starting an IV on your patient before surgery or the patient filling out her intake form in your office. It's not going to help if you demand they do things faster. Take a deep breath and remember that patience is a virtue.

INTUITION

Most doctors will tell you that there were times when they couldn't put their finger on something, but they just had a feeling that something wasn't quite right. I'll give you an example from when I was a resident. I was walking (all right, practically running) out of the hospital and through the emergency room at about 6:30 p.m. after being on call, when a nurse said to me, "Hey, you're neurosurgery. I've got a patient here who's got a problem, and I can't locate the neurosurgical resident who's on call." She had the sixth sense of something bad, and when I saw the patient, so did I.

I went to see him, and he was complaining of a headache. He was at his son's baseball game, and someone threw a ball that accidentally hit him in the head. He was knocked down, but he wasn't knocked unconscious. He had a headache so bad that he came to the emergency room.

I looked at him and knew we needed to get a scan right away. He really looked uncomfortable, pale, and diaphoretic. So instead of just ordering the CT and leaving, I stayed with him. I called the CT tech and told her we had a patient who needed a scan immediately. She said that there was no one there to transport him, so I rolled him to the scanner myself and helped put him on the table. I waited while the images came up and was shocked to find the largest epidural hematoma I'd ever seen. When I went to take him off the table for the scan, he was unconscious with a blown pupil. We took him to surgery right away and removed the blood clot. The guy woke up and was fine. I would say that the intuition of the nurse who directed me to grab the patient and take a look at him saved his life. That was easily something that could have killed this man very quickly.

Things aren't always what you see directly. If that nurse hadn't sensed something wasn't quite right with the man, if we had simply done things by the book, he probably wouldn't have survived. I've seen several patients over the years with similar problems who did not survive. He had a very bad problem, and it was only because we directly took care of it that he was able to get out of that potentially fatal situation.

INSPIRATION

Physicians must have something that stimulates us to do this job. Personally, I'm inspired to get up and go to work every day to do something that might be a little bit bigger than myself. For all of us, just being inspired to help people is what it's all about. Bring that feeling to the job so that you inspire people to want to work around you and with you as well.

When I was a resident, there was a physician named Bob on our staff who really embodied my perception of what an altruistic physician should be. Like the nurse who prevented a head injury fatality, Bob was always willing to take the extra step and be there when he didn't have to and worked extra hard to get the job done. He was very inspiring to me—he's a person whom I've aimed to be more like, trying to emulate the commitment he's had throughout his career.

LOYALTY

You have to be loyal to the people who work for you, and you have to stand by them. That way, you can trust them to stand by you when the time comes. Because loyalty inspires a well-functioning team, it's important for doctors working in a team environment to inspire loyalty among their staff—for themselves, the people around them, and, ultimately, their patients.

FAIRNESS

Everyone wants to be treated fairly. One of the reasons people might be disgruntled with whatever job they have is because they feel like they've been treated unfairly. We should apply uniform standards for how we treat our employees. Make the rules and ensure that everyone abides by them, and when you don't abide by the rules, there will be consequences. It goes without saying that if everyone isn't treated with a standard level of fairness, then there's going to be unhappy people. As an aside, if you don't play by the rules yourself, people will notice—they always do—and you will lose their respect. One of the very important principles regarding this is to set expectations early on in the relationship you have with your employees. These are your responsibilities, and here are ours. Here are the consequences should you fail to meet them, and here are ours. Having this spelled out can save an incredible amount of stress and money in the long run.

RESPECT

On a similar note, everyone who we come in contact with, from patients to team members, should feel respected. It needs to be something that you actually think about, because no one wants to be disrespected. High-level executives and physicians in particular should aspire to that.

I once worked with a physician at a hospital who left a patient's room and said, loudly enough for the patient to hear, "Get him out of here." It was disrespectful to everyone—the patients and also the staff. The staff is tasked with having to deal with this patient, who's clearly been insulted. Maybe the patient was unruly to begin with, but the repercussions of speaking about someone that way are great— from dealing with the family who's upset at the level of disrespect to their family member to suffering the consequences of the patient going home and talking about that experience with everyone they know. I heard somewhere once that if people have a good experience, they will tell two or three people. But if it's a bad experience, they will practically scream it to eleven to fifteen people. It's a lot easier to put people down these days, too, as a result of social media. Imagine if that patient had related that story to all their friends on Facebook or Twitter!

CONSISTENCY

Consistency, consistency, consistency. In everything you do, consistency is key. You don't want to fly off the handle one moment, then become the picture of calmness the next. People want to know what to expect from you, so you must deliver your best on a regular basis.

For example, I try to run a pretty consistent schedule, working from 7:00 or 7:30 a.m. to 5:00 p.m. and having dinner at home at least five nights a week. Work gets done when it's supposed to get done. Both at home and at work, it's important to let people know what to expect, and then following through on that is vital. With a consistent attitude at home, a consistent work environment should follow naturally.

> PEOPLE WANT TO KNOW WHAT TO EXPECT FROM YOU, SO YOU MUST DELIVER YOUR BEST ON A REGULAR BASIS.

EFFORT

One of my favorite sayings is, "How you do anything is how you do everything." It really says it all. Translating that to my industry, to really be a high-level functioning physician or executive, you need to put in your best effort at all times. As a physician, you need to follow through with your best effort at all times—your patients will expect nothing less of you. As a surgeon, I keep going until the job is done.

What kind of effort do you display when you are off work? If you only empty the dishwasher halfway, that's not good enough, and that kind of effort (or lack thereof) could bleed into your work life. If you slack off, you're going to get poor results, and everyone else is going to know it as well.

FAITH

Whatever kind of faith you choose to have, I think we all need to have some sort of belief system. Faith and spirituality can mean all kinds of things, in and outside of religion, and it's my belief that we all benefit from having a reason for being. Otherwise, why are we doing any of this?

At the deep core of your own personality, you must have a reason for wanting to be in a position like that of a physician, and that reason is to help people. You have to have something there that keeps you motivated to do that. For me, I want people to have happier existences based on whatever it is I can do to make them feel better or function better. And at the core of it, I do have that faith. For me, that's what faith means.

GRATITUDE

So many people don't have opportunities to excel in life because of the luck of the draw. They don't have families to love and support them. For many physicians, things have worked out in our favor. I've worked hard over the course of my career to do what I do and to do it well, but I'm lucky too. I was lucky to be born into a family that kept a roof over my head and supported my every pursuit. As Earl Nightingale said, "Luck is what happens when preparedness meets opportunity." Being grateful for that keeps me from getting too big of an ego, and I think most people would benefit from that attitude as well—especially doctors.

Having an attitude of gratitude is what keeps you grounded. I've seen too many doctors who seem to take it all for granted: the respect you get from society, the privileges that are afforded to you, and the income. When I get too far away from this, I pull out a book called *Workers* by Sebastião Salgado; I page through it to see the difficult lives that so many of the people in this world are living. It's very grounding.

SACRIFICE

It goes without saying that most doctors have sacrificed an awful lot to achieve what they've achieved in their careers. It's a time commitment, it's an effort commitment, and it costs a lot of money to become a physician. Sacrifice is inherent in the position, really. The biggest for me was sacrificing my twenties. The amount of work and time and effort that I put into my training during that time frame—from twenty-five to the time I was about thirty-three—was just an enormous amount. And going through my last year of medical school and my seven years of residency was certainly a sacrifice. It has paid off in dividends, but it was really costly, in a number of ways. And young doctors should be prepared for that kind of sacrifice.

TOLERANCE

Physicians have to tolerate a lot, from employees' lack of help to lack of concern or consideration for our time and efforts. I've received inconsiderate phone calls in the middle of the night from nurses saying, "I think we should tell you about this even though we don't want you to do anything about it until tomorrow morning." Why wake up a doctor at 3 a.m. if it isn't urgent? Once I received a call from a patient at 7 a.m. on a Sunday morning, waking me up. (Those were the days when I could sleep in.) She wanted me to refill her prescription—for what, I don't remember. Rather than prolong the discussion, I said, "Fine, what's the number? I'll call them right now." She said, "Oh, they don't open until 9 a.m." Grrrr.

Or a team member may say, "So-and-so didn't do their job, so I think I need you to come in here and take care of this." These scenarios are a daily part of the job, so you must have a strong sense of tolerance in order to, well, tolerate it. You simply have to shrug your shoulders and accept it; be grateful—as you remember, another key value—for what you have and then just move on. Otherwise, you really become bitter and resentful, and that's no way to live your life.

INTEGRITY

Integrity, for me, is identifying these values we are describing here and then living them—every single day. Being true to your values is what having integrity is all about. Treating your family, your staff, and your patients with respect is a form of integrity. But saying you'll treat them with respect, and then turning your back on them when they need support, is not really showing integrity. Identifying your values and then standing by those values no matter what is what it means to exhibit integrity.

* * *

When it comes to the types of attitudes and the types of thought processes that high-level, peak professionals exhibit, demonstrating all of these values is going to help you live a better, happier, stress-free life. For example, being able to shrug your shoulders, take things for what they are, and just move on is generally the best move. It's not worth the agony of trying to change everyone, make them bend to you.

I want to be a high-level, functioning person. I want people to look at me and say, "This guy has got his act together. He treats people well. He doesn't act like he's better than anybody else." And for me, these qualities are the ones I feel help me reach that goal.

What do you want people to think about you?

BEN FRANKLIN'S VALUES

Speaking of values, Ben Franklin had some opinions on the subject too. I always find myself returning to these principles I read about many years ago.

In early adulthood, Ben Franklin resolved to achieve moral perfection, a very lofty goal! He wrote in his autobiography about how he developed these values and would consider each one for a week at a time, completing the cycle four times each year. Although these values seem a bit archaic over two hundred years later, the concept of striving to improve yourself is timeless. Here they are:

- Temperance. Eat not to dullness; drink not to elevation.

- Silence. Speak not but what may benefit others or yourself; avoid trifling conversation.

- Order. Let all your things have their places; let each part of your business have its time.

- Resolution. Resolve to perform what you ought; perform without fail what you resolve.

- Frugality. Make no expense but to do good to others or yourself; i.e., waste nothing.

- Industry. Lose no time; be always employ'd [sic] in something useful; cut off all unnecessary actions.

- Sincerity. Use no hurtful deceit; think innocently and justly, and, if you speak, speak accordingly.

- Justice. Wrong none by doing injuries, or omitting the benefits that are your duty.

- Moderation. Avoid extremes; forbear resenting injuries so much as you think they deserve.

- Cleanliness. Tolerate no uncleanliness in body, clothes, or habitation.

- Tranquillity [sic]. Be not disturbed at trifles, or at accidents common or unavoidable.

- Chastity. Rarely use venery but for health or offspring, never to dullness, weakness, or the injury of your own or another's peace or reputation.

- Humility. Imitate Jesus and Socrates.

ACTION STEPS

1. Write down your top ten personal and professional values. From these, and your plans for the future, develop your personal vision and mission statements. Here are some ideas on how to help you get started:

   - Write down about twenty-five core values (it's easy to find a list of dozens of these values online).

   - Whittle these down to your top seven to ten (more than this is hard to keep track of).

- Incorporate these into your vision statement: this is the view of your ideal world—how you think things should be for you and the people around you.

- Use your vision statement to craft your mission statement as a physician. It should be short and succinct, the reason being that you will need to communicate this to your staff, and no one will remember a long-winded statement. It should be something like, "We at Acme Medicine are dedicated to providing professional pulmonary service to our patients in a caring, respectful manner."

- Write it down, and put it on the wall for you and your staff to see every day.

- Then live it.

CHAPTER 5

FOUNDATION THREE

Communication

Communication, the human connection, is
the key to personal and career success.
—Paul J. Meyer

W hen I finished training, I thought: "I'm a good communicator—I can relate to patients and their families.
I can communicate with the operating room [OR]
staff and office personnel." It's true, I was a lot better
than some other surgeons I knew, and I had a busy practice and was
doing the type of surgery I enjoyed.

Yet something was missing. I was uncomfortable talking to
patients except in the most specific terms relating to their problems.
I disliked social and networking events. I could never remember

people's names. Public speaking (aside from giving a lecture about a neurosurgical topic) made me very uncomfortable, and I had difficulty communicating my needs in business settings. I heard somewhere that public speaking came in ahead of death in a survey of people's fears—that meant they'd rather be lying in a wake than giving the eulogy. I was that guy! Spending so much time studying and trying to excel in our chosen profession leaves precious little time to improve soft skills like communication.

I once worked with a doctor who was seemingly angry all the time. We'll call him Dr. Irate. He was mad at the office staff (they "never scheduled good patients" for him); he was mad at his colleagues (they "just didn't respond" to his requests for consultations or asked him to consult "inappropriately"); he was mad at the OR staff (his cases "were not scheduled correctly," they "never had the right equipment," etc.); and he was mad at his patients (amazing!). He was angry at the government and the insurance companies who made his life difficult and reduced his income.

As you might imagine, he did not enjoy a happy reputation among his peers, and he was not (and still isn't) alone. I've met several doctors during my career who've had similar attitudes. They are difficult to deal with, and I can't imagine what their patients think. The staff dislikes them and gossips behind their backs. One of them told me, "Oh, I know I'm being an asshole; that's the only way to get things done around here." Really? How can such physicians possibly enjoy their career choice?

When I was growing up, a manager at the fast food restaurant where I worked told me, "No one is without self-worth—you can always be used as a bad example." Dr. Irate (and several others I have met through the years) taught me the truth in that statement. In my case, I began to study communication topics in some detail, reading about related subjects and attending seminars on negotiation and communication strategies. In talking to other doctors, I soon recognized how common such problems are among the medical community.

You may be asking (like I did), "Why is communication so important? I have all these degrees, so isn't it obvious how smart I am? Shouldn't that be enough?" These are legitimate questions, but as we all know, "They don't care how much you know until they know how much you care."

So how do you communicate how much you care?

The difficulty we face is the fact that we need to be able to communicate with people from all walks of life and in every possible situation. Examples include one-on-one counseling of patients about health problems, ranging from the most simple and mundane to very private and sensitive topics to the most complicated and life-threatening situations; networking at a specialty function; discussing employee absenteeism; negotiating fees with an insurance company giant; and dealing with our own defiant teenagers. (Come to think of it, there may not be such a big difference in that last comparison.)

So how should physicians go about becoming better communicators? It's best to begin with a bit of goal setting.

BECOMING A BETTER COMMUNICATOR

1. Set Goals
2. Be Proactive
3. Persevere

I. SET GOALS

I knew I needed to work on my communication skills when I realized I was never getting my way. If you're not getting your way, take responsibility. In some sense, you are allowing people to take advantage of you. Don't assume that it's always the other person's fault. (After all, everyone's favorite radio station is WIIFM: What's In It for Me.) People aren't out to get other people unless they've been wronged. If you find that someone is trying to mess with you constantly, you might want to think about how you're treating them and say, "Well, maybe I'm just going to twist this around and turn it into something positive."

That's something that I really started to consciously and intentionally think about, but it took a long time for me to come to that conclusion. Here are a few communication goals I learned to set for myself, and I continue to work toward these principles every day.

COMMUNICATION GOALS:
1. Be Skeptical ... of Yourself
2. Be Friendly
3. Have Empathy
4. Learn to Negotiate

1. Be Skeptical ... of Yourself

As a young physician, you'll find that people will be skeptical of you. They realize that you don't know it all. You don't realize that, but they do. And you have to be careful with how you communicate at that stage of your career until you develop a sense of reading other people. Ask yourself, "Am I getting through to this person? Does it appear that what I'm saying is making sense to them?" Ask yourself those questions whether you're talking to nurses in the hospital, people on your staff, patients, or patients' families, and don't just stop once you're established in your practice. If you find that there are perhaps frequent misunderstandings, consider asking yourself if the problem is with yourself or with others.

When you're in a conversation with someone, are they fidgeting around? Are they paying attention to you? Do you have a sense that they're plotting some revenge against you? Really effective leaders don't just barge in and scream orders at people. They figure out what that person wants, and they try to tie what they need with what the other person wants.

2. Be Friendly

There's a physician who joined our group a few years back, and nothing seemed to go right for this guy. He had a lot of complaints about the staff, he complained about working late, he never could get his cases scheduled on time, he had the worst patients, and so forth and so on. But it was all the fault of the doctor, who ordered people around like a dictator.

Because of his bad leadership, his team didn't want to do anything he said. If he'd have been nice, if he'd treated them with respect, the whole operation would have run more smoothly, and the doctor could have been able to go home—maybe even early—with a smile on his face every day. Needless to say, he's moved on. I'm skeptical life is any better for him in his new position.

3. Have Empathy

One critical skill for a physician is empathy. Why? Because if you simply throw facts and figures out to people (staff, patients, family), they will buck you at every turn. I read somewhere recently that people don't want to be *told* things—they resist. You have to read them, to bring them along to your way of thinking, to your conclusion, your diagnosis, your treatment plan. You have to be able to say, "Hey, I'm talking to this person, but they're looking away from me; they're playing with their phones; they're staring into space; they're giving me monotone, one-word answers. Maybe there's something wrong with the way I'm communicating."

Being able to empathize with someone else's predicament is important in becoming a good leader, so try to read others better and have a heart for what someone may be going through. Communicate that they matter—that's how to communicate like a good leader.

4. Learn to Negotiate

When I set out to become a better communicator, I went to a course on negotiation. Really, I didn't know it would teach me about communication, per se, but what I did learn is that virtually everything that we have or want or need in life is controlled or owned by other people. And if we don't have a good way of communicating with these people, we're probably going to have a hard time getting the things that we want. So that was actually pretty helpful to me, because I had merely thought I'd learn about how to negotiate a contract. That's what we think about when we think about negotiations, right? But virtually every interaction we have with other people involves some sort of negotiation.

For example:

"Where do you want to go to lunch?"

"Oh, let's go to the pizza place."

"No, I don't want to go there."

"Well, why not? And where else can we go?"

Or:

"Mr. Jones, you have a herniated disc. I think we should operate."

"Well, I don't want to have surgery."

"Why not?"

"I can't afford it right now."

"I can have my insurance expert talk to you about how we can help."

"It's not that. I can't take off work right now."

"OK, let's see if we can figure out something else to get you some relief."

What I learned during that course helped me in my patient care too, because as a doctor, you listen to a story of a patient and you formulate a diagnosis, trying to think about what can be done to treat whatever problem they're having. But again, that's a form of negotiation. You're going to make sure the patient has a prescription plan where that medication is not going to cost $500 a month. Because if it does, they're not going to get it. So you're going to have to talk to them and negotiate some solution that will work for them. You think that the patient needs surgery, and they don't agree. OK, is there something else that can work for treating this problem, whatever it is?

> BEING A GOOD NEGOTIATOR MEANS UNDERSTANDING THAT PEOPLE DON'T WANT THE SAME THINGS, BUT EVERYONE HAS CERTAIN NEEDS AND WANTS.

People don't want the same things. If you're trying to buy a car, for example, you may think that everything depends on the price, but that might not actually be the case. If you walk into a car dealership on the last day of the month, the salesman really wants the sale. Let's say he doesn't care how much he makes on it—he just has to have another number on the books for the month. Being a good nego-tiator means understanding that people don't want the same things, but everyone has certain needs and wants. Trying to figure out how your needs and wants fit into others' was really not something that I thought about before.

These are just some of the challenges we face in communicat-ing on a regular basis. To my knowledge, doctors have very little formal training in this important field of study, and yet, our ability to achieve success in most fields is critically dependent on our ability to make our own needs, wants, and desires known and to discern the same for others. So there is a gap. I'll touch on negotiating a little more in the next chapter as well.

2. BE PROACTIVE

Learning to communicate better doesn't begin and end with this book. You must proactively seek out further resources to help you along the way. That's what I've done.

I've read books and journals, attended seminars and workshops, watched videos, and listened to podcasts about how to be a better communicator. And oftentimes, such endeavors are also opportuni-ties to network and practice newfound skills.

Of all the resources I've sought out, I found Dale Carnegie's course on effective communication to be one of the most beneficial programs I have taken over the years. Carnegie wrote *How to Win Friends and Influence People*, and the course revolves around prin-ciples from the book.

Developing a new habit can take many weeks of repetition (I've seen ranges from 21 to 250 days). Because the Carnegie course runs 12 weeks, many of the techniques become ingrained and therefore more likely to persist after the course ends. Instead of just learning something out of a book or watching someone at a seminar and spending a day or two on it, it was something that we studied and practiced weekly over that three-month period.

What did we learn in the course? How to approach people in a friendly way, how to be good listeners, how to ease tensions, and how to stand up in front of a crowd to deliver a talk with no props or PowerPoint presentations to hide behind. We learned how to talk in terms of others' interests, ask questions rather than give orders, develop empathy, and see things from others' viewpoints, among other things. At times, it was difficult. I was no different than others at that time in my dislike of public speaking.

In working through the course, we spent time on many of these concepts. We learned the effect that applying these ideas had on people and the value in establishing good relationships.

The psychology behind Carnegie's philosophies is as effective today as it was almost a hundred years ago. People want certain things out of life. Everyone wants to be appreciated. Everybody wants some recognition for what they've done and some appreciation for their accomplishments.

I was about to board a plane to Charlotte one day and was then going to transfer to a flight to New York. We had just done this one part of the Dale Carnegie course on smiling. My flight to Charlotte ended up getting canceled, but I needed to get to New York. I was picking my wife up there, and we were going to have dinner and go to a show for Valentine's Day.

Long story short, I ended up getting to Charlotte about two hours late, after my connection left. When we got there, I was told to go to the help desk, where another flight could be arranged for me. I imagined that the airport employees were probably really badly abused that day, but I wanted to treat them with kindness. I went up there, remembering what we'd just learned in the Dale Carnegie course, and I smiled. I asked the staff member helping me, "How are things going?"

He kind of shrugged and said, "Not so great. We've got all these flights canceled. People are being reboarded, reticketed."

I said, "I know; I'm trying to get up there for dinner with my wife for Valentine's Day." Then I smiled again and said, "I'm sorry your day's so bad with all the stuff going on." He ended up getting me reboarded, so I thanked him, told him I hoped his day got better, and walked away. It turned out that not only did he get me on the next flight out, but he put me in first class.

That just never would've happened if I hadn't taken a little bit of time to be sociable with the guy. I was not demanding like most people are when they get stressed out by flight cancellation chaos. That moment taught me a great lesson in defusing problems, and that's pretty valuable. It would've never happened if I hadn't taken the Dale Carnegie course, where we were forced to smile at people as part of negotiation tactics. So that's just one way that I have found that being proactive at becoming a better communicator has had very positive effects—that lesson is now part of my everyday behavior.

But that's not necessarily easy. It takes perseverance.

3. PERSEVERE

After finding the right resources for you, take what you learn and apply your newfound principles at every opportunity.

Every interaction you have with another person is an opportunity to take some of the lessons you've learned and put them into practice. If you're sitting at a seminar, or you're at a coffee shop, try to ask yourself, "What kind of day is this person having behind the counter there? Maybe there's something that I can say to make their day a little bit brighter." Then try to hone the skills that you're learning because there's nothing that's going to take the place of continued practice.

I've continued to practice communication skills by attending Toastmasters, the international society that teaches effective communication and leadership skills. Most people come to Toastmasters without any public speaking skills at all (that was me), but it's not just public speaking; it's all kinds of speaking. Most of the groups meet every couple of weeks for an hour or so. It's a very low-cost and minimal time investment. At each meeting, members have the opportunity to give a five- to ten-minute speech, and then they get evaluated by the other members of the club. The other members will tell them things like, "You could make better eye contact," or "You need to use hand gestures a little bit more effectively," or "You should not be so stationary behind the podium," or "You need to stop saying the word *like* every other word."

You can use these techniques to get better at what you do, and that doesn't apply just to standing in front of a crowd. It applies to any situation. Suppose you're at a meeting or talking to a patient or their family—how are you going to best get your points across?

Toastmasters is a great resource, because it's a voluntary meeting every other week that allows you to progressively work on your communication. Nobody's going to put a rope around your neck and say you have to talk next week. The reason you're there is to get better, so at every opportunity that I can attend one of these meetings, I do, because I want to get better. I want to get more comfortable standing in front of a crowd. The repetition is the thing that does it for me. You can't just read about how to go in front of a crowd and use your hands effectively. Reading about it is one thing, but when you're standing up there, it's very easy just to hide behind the podium, not make eye contact with anybody, and just look at your slides. If you do it every week, or every other week, and somebody is critiquing you and saying, "Look, you're hiding behind the podium; you have got to come out from there," then you will inevitably get better and better. You have to persevere and keep trying.

* * *

If you really want to be an effective speaker and communicator, then those are some of the things that you need to do: set goals, be proactive, and persevere.

With goals, good resources, and persistence, you can only get better. And it's repetition that really helps you more than anything else—it's the difference between a doctor who's read about a certain surgery and a doctor who has performed it a hundred times. It simply stands to reason that the person who's done it a hundred times is going to be a lot better than the person who just read about it (at least, I hope so).

What will be your first goal in becoming a better communicator?

ACTION STEPS

1. Set a goal to become a better communicator.

2. Read books like *How to Win Friends and Influence People*, *Crucial Conversations*, and *Effective Negotiation*.

3. Check out some TED Talks on communication.

4. Take a seminar like the Dale Carnegie course.

5. Join a local Toastmasters club.

6. Apply the principles you learn at every opportunity—
    they will change your life. They did mine!

CHAPTER 6

FOUNDATION THREE

Communication: Leadership Roles

Communication is the real work of leadership.
—Nitin Nohria, dean of Harvard Business School

magine hiring a young physician who looks so good on paper that you bypass what should be the standard procedure of introducing him to the high standards of your practice. Instead of a proper orientation, complete with communicating to him the company's overall mission and giving fair warning of what is expected in order to ensure a professional environment, you simply assume he knows how things work in your practice. You send him out without any instructions or supervision, and you learn the hard way that he's a slacker on whom no one can depend. You find out too late, after the staff have grown weary of this person, that he has to go. He isn't a good fit, and now you must waste time and money on recruiting another doctor. If only you'd gotten him on the same page as everyone else from day one. Unfortunately, this kind of thing happens far too often. It's happened to me at least twice in my own practice, and I've seen it many times in other groups. (Not with me; I wasn't the slacker who didn't fit in.)

Now imagine a situation where you are the one interviewing for a position. You know what kind of practice you wish to join, and you find one that seemingly fits the bill. Then you discover that things aren't so rosy after all. The staff isn't happy, the physicians work long hours, and there's no plan to develop your practice. Do you walk away, or do you sit down with the principles and try to collectively develop a plan to make this your dream practice? Being able to communicate in an effective and ethical manner here might be the key.

Having good communication skills is just generally going to make your life easier, but especially in the office or hospital. From knowing how to manage your staff with the right set of rules communicated from the start to negotiating with insurance companies, communicating effectively will always serve you. In this chapter, we'll first look at some of the settings where those skills will come in handy before we delve into seven ways leaders in the medical field can be more effective.

> FROM KNOWING HOW TO MANAGE YOUR STAFF WITH THE RIGHT SET OF RULES COMMUNICATED FROM THE START TO NEGOTIATING WITH INSURANCE COMPANIES, COMMUNICATING EFFECTIVELY WILL ALWAYS SERVE YOU.

THE WHERE

Here are the settings where effective communication would most benefit doctors both at home and at work. What settings best apply to you?

Clinics, Hospitals, and Operating Rooms

In my experience, I've seen surgeons who aren't very effective in developing team structures for surgical procedures. What that leads to is a lot of disgruntled staff who don't want to work with those surgeons. An important part of a surgical procedure has to do with the surgeon leading the team, and that definitely involves taking a perspective on what it is you're doing and why you are there in the operating room. If you find that a certain staff member doesn't quite grasp what you're doing or why you're doing it, then it's incumbent upon you, as the surgeon, to teach them.

Hospital and Community Leadership Roles

As medicine changes, there are challenges and opportunities for doctors to take the lead and focus a hospital team's efforts over the next six months, year, or five-year time frame. I think physicians ought to be the ones to lead this rather than hospital administrators.

I heard a marketer once say, "People are just walking around with an umbilical cord and they want to plug it in to somebody and have somebody tell them what to do." I think there's a lot of truth in that in the sense that people do want to be told what's good for them and what isn't good for them. Physicians are in a unique position to do this because they have more advanced training in a lot of different things than most of the population. More surgeons should take an active role in the direction of their communities and of the hospital they serve as well.

Community Education and Practice Building

Any doctor who wants to be known as an expert in their field could benefit from building up their reputation within the community. And a lot of patients and their families are interested in learning directly about how to diagnose what the best treatments are for anything from arthritis of the knee to diabetes. Many hospitals offer opportunities, like community education programs, so being able to deliver an effective talk to the public in a meaningful way can go a long way toward establishing yourself as an expert in this area. And once you've established yourself as an expert, you may find yourself giving lectures and being seen as somewhat of a little celebrity in your community. That can enhance your standing and will help with instilling patients' trust in you. That's great for your career, and it's also great for your referral business.

Family

Communication at home means asking yourself, "How are we going to function as a family?" Everyone wants to raise healthy and well-adjusted people, but it doesn't just *happen*. It has to be communicated on a regular basis. One of my mentors sets aside a weekly date night with his wife. It's a sacred time for them to go out; discuss concerns, problems, and plans; and just generally have an enjoyable evening. Great idea!

I have a couple of daughters, and one of them is particularly prone to getting hangry—angry because she's hungry. It's easy to just snap back at her, and I had a habit of doing this, but that makes things worse, and then everyone is upset. And so over a period of time I've learned that maybe the first thing to do is to make sure this kid is well fed before I start snapping back. (As an aside here, I also realized where she got this from: me! I can be a jerk when I'm hungry, especially to servers. To combat this, I eat something before I go out to dinner—this helps a lot!) Taking a deep breath and trying to figure out little things like this is really helpful toward building a harmonious life.

SEVEN WAYS LEADERS CAN BE MORE EFFECTIVE

Effective communication will empower you as a leader and help your business run more smoothly. Here are seven leadership roles for which you'll need excellent communication skills:

1. Communicating with patients
2. Communicating with staff
3. Interacting with other doctors in your own practice
4. Negotiating
5. Attending networking events
6. Teaching medical students, residents, and young physicians
7. Community education and practice building

1. Communicating with Patients

Communicating well and effectively with patients is the difference between a great doctor and a terrible one. You can be a better communicator by developing listening strategies, establishing trust, and knowing how to speak to patients in a way that is understandable and not full of medical jargon.

Developing Listening Strategies

We always talk about being a good listener, but what does that mean? According to a study published in the *Journal of General Internal Medicine*, doctors listen to a patient's reason for visiting for an average of eleven seconds before interrupting the patient.[2] That's not enough time to really get a good feel for what's going on. So as I have progressed more in my career, I have spent more time listening to what patients have to say rather than talking or looking at scans and relying on that to make a diagnosis. Just because there is radiographic evidence of a diagnosis doesn't mean that is the problem that brought the patient to your office.

Establishing Trust

When it comes to patient-doctor relationships, the most important thing that you can do is establish enough trust that the patient relies on you, the doctor, for advice and recommendations. Patients will look at you and unconsciously evaluate you, asking themselves if you're a good listener, if you are knowledgeable, if you really care, if you're relevant to them.

How you communicate through your body language and the amount of face time you give them goes a long way toward establishing the trust that you need to have. You have to have these patients on your side in order to deliver an effective treatment for them.

---

2 Naykky Singh Ospina, et al., "Eliciting the Patient's Agenda—Secondary Analysis of Recorded Clinical Encounters," *Journal of General Internal Medicine* 34, (July 2, 2018): 36–40, https://doi.org/10.1007/s11606-018-4540-5.

Communicating Diagnosis, Prognosis, and Treatment Plan

It's well known that the average patient is not particularly versed on the medical jargon physicians use. I once worked with a physician assistant who was a smart guy; he knew what he was doing, but he would talk to patients and their families as if they really understood some of the very complicated terminology that we use when we're talking to each other. He'd show them an MRI scan and say, "So here we can see there is some lateral recess stenosis around the L4 nerve root. It's due to ligamentous and facet hypertrophy. I think it explains your L4 radiculopathy. So if we do a limited laminectomy and medial facetectomy, I think your pain is likely to go away." Say what? And so the patients would walk out confused, and a lot of times they didn't follow the treatment plan because, frankly, they couldn't understand it. I'm not sure I understood it sometimes. They'd wind up with another doctor, or they'd insist on coming back and talking to me directly. This was not an efficient use of time in our practice.

Patients need to know that you have thought about everything that they've presented to you in a meaningful way. Then they need to know that you've come up with a diagnosis and a treatment plan, which you should be communicating in a way that helps them understand what's happening. They're going to be much more likely to follow your directions if they know what it is you're telling them to do and why.

2. Communicating with Staff

Managing staff in your clinic, hospital, and operating or procedure room in a way that is effective comes down to communicating your overall mission to them and hiring the perfect liaisons to help communicate to staff and handle personnel issues.

Establish Overall Mission

I saw a lecture by former Notre Dame football coach Lou Holtz, and he spoke about motivating his players at the beginning of the season. He told them that every player had a role and that every player knew what the goal was and could work together well, knowing how their individual roles would affect the end result—his team eventually, in 1988, won the national championship.

Like any sports team, everyone in a physician's office has a role in the overall goal, which in our case is the delivery of good patient care, and it starts when that patient picks up the phone to make their first appointment with our scheduler. When the patient arrives, the receptionist checks the patient in. The medical assistant then takes the vital signs and gathers a brief medical history, and then the patient is in the hands of the physician assistant, the doctor, and finally the checkout receptionist.

All these employees have a role, and they need to know that it's part of a big picture. The person who answers the phone needs to understand that their role is not to just robotically answer the phone and transfer the call to someone else. The patient needs to know that they're being cared for and that this is just part of that caring process. When these things are done, the patients are much more satisfied with the overall experience they've had, and the staff is more likely to be happy in their jobs because they know that they're part of a bigger thing and that they're an important part of the delivery of that care.

Get an Office Manager You Trust (but Verify Them First)

We'll discuss this further at the end of the book, but I wanted to point out here how crucial it is to have an office manager who's a good communicator. This person is the liaison between you and the rest of the office and frequently will troubleshoot problems with patients.

An office manager can ensure staff are aware of their roles within the framework of the business. That person is also the one who'll be aware of staff sensitivity skills and can handle personnel issues, like hiring, firing, and training.

The office manager can make a huge difference by hiring the right people with the right attitude and by making sure that the staff has a good understanding of the company's daily communications expectations. This is especially important in an office like mine, where I'm not there all the time because I'm in surgery. But I do like to spend time with my staff to make sure they understand that I appreciate what they're doing.

3. Interacting with Other Doctors in Your Own Practice

When it comes to interacting with other physicians within your own practice, you must be a good negotiator and learn to firmly establish standards and hold people accountable to ensure a professional environment.

Establish Standards

It's important to establish standards with in-house colleagues from the start, getting on the same page about everything from interacting with other staff and responding to pages or calls in a timely manner to following charting and electronic medical records guidelines and solving problems both effectively and independently.

We had a doctor in our practice who was consistently late. As a result, he was not only a bad leader, but he also created an environment that led to a lot of unhappy people. The patients weren't happy and the staff wasn't happy about having to cover for this other person.

Though it would seem obvious that being on time is an expectation of the business, the importance of being on time and consequences of being late should have been made clear from the beginning. In my experience, expectations need to be spelled out to people. No matter what level of training or education someone has had, expectations should be made clear, well ahead of time, to avoid conflict later on. That's the way in which effective communication needs to be used within a practice—it needs to be done up front.

Hold People Accountable to Ensure a Professional Environment

After establishing standards, be sure to follow through, holding people accountable and ensuring a professional environment. That might mean firing someone because they don't live up to the standards you've already established. Besides the desire to have an office full of happy people and an operation that runs smoothly, there's also the cost of recruiting that should be considered. If you set the standard from the start and consistently hold every hire accountable, you'll waste less time and money in hiring and recruiting. It makes much more sense to outline the expectations even before you hire and to, for example, give new hires a ninety-day trial period.

> A BAD COMMUNICATOR CANNOT BE A GOOD NEGOTIATOR, AND EFFECTIVE NEGOTIATIONS ARE KEY WHEN IT COMES TO COMMUNICATING WITH PARTNERS, ASSOCIATES, AND OTHER PROFESSIONALS.

4. Negotiating

A bad communicator cannot be a good negotiator, and effective negotiations are key when it comes to communicating with partners, associates, and other professionals. Here are some of the areas in which being a good negotiator will make your life so much easier.

Consultations

When a fellow physician phones the office to schedule a consultation for whatever reason, it helps to know how to negotiate your way through that process. Spend time getting the details of the potential patient over the phone, and determine if it's the right fit or if the patient should perhaps be seen by someone else. Being able to communicate those things with other physicians in a meaningful way will lead to less conflict and make things a lot easier on everyone.

Business-Related Practice Issues and Discussions with Potential and Existing Partners and Associates

As far as business-related practice issues go, financial questions tend to arise, such as, "Do we need to buy this piece of equipment?" or "Should we extend the rent on this office building that we're in, or should we think about building our own office building?" Or even HR questions like, "Is this a staff member that we need to counsel more, or are they at the end of their time here and they need to be let go?" Being a good communicator will help you negotiate your way through these types of scenarios.

We have to negotiate with our partners and our employees, fielding concerns like, "Are we hiring this person?" or "How much are we paying them?" or "Are they negotiating their benefits?" Honing negotiation skills will help alleviate the stress of these inevitable conversations.

Hospital Administrations

If you're involved in a hospital in any way, you may have issues with the administration, in which case negotiation skills can be your friend. Such skills can help you deal with issues like needing a piece of equipment that only the hospital can afford, and the piece of equipment has to live in the hospital. Maybe it's an X-ray machine or some piece of specialized equipment for surgery, and the hospital wants to know how this is going to benefit your patients and what their return on their investment is going to be. Don't be stuck without negotiation skills in times like these.

Insurance Companies

Knowing how to communicate effectively with the insurance company is crucial, as it can mean the difference between getting a test or a surgery approved or denied. Learning how to communicate and negotiate in important situations like this (and training your staff to do this as well) can seriously reduce conflict with insurance representatives, and doing a good job also increases the chance that you're going to eventually get whatever it was that you wanted in the first place.

> KNOWING HOW TO SOCIALIZE IN A MEANINGFUL WAY AND HOW TO NETWORK CAN MEAN MEETING THE RIGHT PERSON TO HELP YOU FURTHER YOUR PRACTICE.

5. Attending Networking Events

Knowing how to socialize in a meaningful way and how to network can mean meeting the right person to help you further your practice. It's a good thing people love to talk about themselves—half the battle is over once you realize this truth.

So how do you network? The next time you're at a work-related event and have trouble striking up conversations, ask people who they are and where they came from, what their families are like, where they live, what they do for hobbies, what they do for fun. You have to take an active interest in other people in order for the conversation to be a good, effective one. Check out Dale Carnegie's book mentioned earlier for some tips on how to be a good conversationalist.

When I was younger and socially awkward, I went to quite a few networking events. I'm not that great at socializing at events even now, but I'm definitely better than I was. Back then, I would be talking to a stranger and they would say, "So, what do you do?" and I would say, "Well, I'm a neurosurgeon." They would be like, "OK," and then wouldn't know where to go with that conversation. And so it was very awkward for everyone. I decided to tell my brother about it, and then one evening he was able to witness this experience himself. He agreed: it was really awkward. What he recommended was to, instead of letting the conversation die there, respond with things like, "Well, what do you do? Where do you live, and where have you lived before? Do you like your job, and what do you like about your job?" I found in turning the conversation around that it was much more comfortable to listen to others than to talk about myself, and people really appreciate being listened to. A lot of people don't really get that, but that's how you do it—it's pretty simple.

6. Teaching Medical Students, Residents, and Young Physicians

Most doctors are awful at giving lectures and pretty much hide behind the slide deck and stand in the corner of the room, just pointing up to the slides. I recently went to a conference with great examples of terrible presentations. One presenter said, "I know this is a busy slide, but here's what I want to point out to you." I thought to myself, "Well, if that's all you wanted to point out on the slide, why didn't you delete 90 percent of that slide and just have what you want in there?" Everything else was useless. This lesson can be applied to teaching medicine too. Don't confuse your audience with unnecessary bullet points. It's important to take the time and examine what makes for an effective presentation. Keep that and eliminate the rest. It's very easy to include everything you've learned, but it's important to visualize the experience from others' viewpoints. What do they *need* to know? What can I eliminate?

7. Community Education and Practice Building

Many hospitals, churches, YMCAs, and community centers will frequently sponsor medical talks. Let's say you wanted to do a talk on knee replacement surgery—think about how to approach that topic in a way that is engaging and comprehensible. Instead of just talking about how to do knee replacement surgery, you might talk about the causes of knee pain and how you can prevent it. And when you do that kind of thing, you establish yourself as an expert, raise your reputation in the community, and help people who may not be able to get the type of medical care you deliver any other way.

* * *

Now let's reimagine hiring a new physician. First of all, there's an office manager in place to do the communicating. This time, the new doc looks great on paper and continues to shine well after the contract is signed, all because she's had what's expected of her clearly communicated to her from the outset. The office manager made sure to get her on the same page as the rest of the office from day one. This makes everything run smoothly, and everyone goes home with big smiles on their faces. You, the happy physician, have the time to focus on developing your own communications skills at networking events, where you've met a community center director who'd like you to present at an upcoming outreach program the center is holding. You're able to negotiate a good time and topic, because you're always working on those skills as well. At the community center, you're able to engage with members of the community who truly appreciate your time and your expertise, which they can clearly understand since you replaced medical jargon with plain ol' English.

Life seems a whole lot easier now, doesn't it?

ACTION STEPS

1. What listening strategy do you use with patients, and how can you improve it?

2. What is your overall mission when hiring employees, and how can you communicate that clearly?

3. How can you improve upon negotiating with insurance companies?

4. Name three to five networking questions that would be useful in your next social interaction.

5. Make some calls and inquire about doing a talk at a community center or hospital in your area of expertise.

6. Practice a presentation on friends and family who are not in the medical field, asking them to look out for ways in which your focus was unclear or the terminology incomprehensible.

CHAPTER 7

FOUNDATION THREE

Communication, Leadership, and Motivation

Before you are a leader, success is about growing yourself. When you become a leader, success is all about growing others.
—Jack Welch, former CEO, General Electric

I n my twenty-five-plus years in practice, I've seen many facets of leadership in action—some great, some good, many bad or awful. I've held leadership roles in my practices, locally in my hospital and regionally (in the Tennessee Neurosurgical Society). I've made plenty of mistakes along the way, and I've seen others undermine their considerable academic accomplishments by treating other people poorly.

Leadership was an important subject in my MBA program, and through these experiences, I've identified five keys to better leadership and motivation in my practice. In turn, these principles have made my practice much better off and more professionally rewarding for me. Those keys are as follows:

1. Know your values

2. Have a vision

3. Be a lifelong learner

4. Be a positive role model

5. Connect

In this chapter, we'll go over these five key principles that will enable you to begin to improve your leadership abilities. The information we will discuss here is by no means comprehensive; however, let it inspire you to learn more and take positive action. These principles will apply whether you have been given a formal leadership role or would never consider such a position. *Even if you are not the president or vice president, you are still a leader.* This comes by nature of your standing as a physician.

EVEN IF YOU ARE NOT THE PRESIDENT OR VICE PRESIDENT, YOU ARE STILL A LEADER. THIS COMES BY NATURE OF YOUR STANDING AS A PHYSICIAN.

In addition to these leadership concepts, we'll talk a bit about motivation. Motivation is also an important part of leadership. We not only have to motivate ourselves but also our staff, our patients, and our community.

So, exactly what is leadership, and how can you apply it to your practice?

Some people view leadership as giving people the tools they need to succeed. Others talk about developing an open and positive influence on their team. Still others describe leadership as building a consensus to get a job done and helping others achieve success.

Most would agree that leadership does not come naturally and has to be worked on regularly. In any case, understanding your role as a leader and working to get better at it is what we will be discussing here.

For me, leadership in medicine is this: having an internal compass that guides you in your daily life and allows you to set a positive example for those around you. True leadership is having a vision for your practice and your patients and communicating that vision in a way that moves people (your staff, your associates, and your patients) forward and gets things done.

In my view, to be an effective, positive leader, you must first consider some internal (self-improvement) moves and then work to improve the way you communicate those things to the world around you. The first three keys—knowing your values, having a vision, and being a lifelong learner—are all internal qualities. Defining and practicing those three key qualities are the first things we will discuss.

Let's get started!

KEYS TO BETTER LEADERSHIP AND MOTIVATION
Key 1: Know Your Values

The quality of a leader is reflected in the standards they set for themselves.
—Ray Kroc

Knowing your values means having a set of values and a moral compass by which you live and being self-aware enough to recognize them and act accordingly. As we go through school and training, we see other people and how they act in different circumstances. Our parents or other role models have shown us how to act and behave as well. We take all these experiences with us, in every action we have with others—some good and some bad.

How many times have we taken the time to sit down and think about what our true values are? These traits are ones that highly regarded leaders exhibit: integrity, respect for others, the courage to act, honesty, and humility. Others include being justice minded and having initiative, enthusiasm, knowledge, good judgment, and decisiveness. The way that you act will reflect your internal values. If your values are strong and positive, your actions will reflect this, and vice versa.

The point here is that your values and moral compass will determine your behavior with respect to the way you treat others. This includes your staff, your peers, your patients, and your family. If you truly believe that you are better than others with respect to your standing in the community or intelligence, that belief will be reflected in your interactions as well and probably not to your benefit. People will feel intimidated in your presence and may be too afraid to share ideas or thoughts that might help you.

Key 2: Have a Vision

Leadership is the capacity to translate vision into reality.
—Warren Bennis

Good leaders have an overall vision for themselves and for others around them. This overall vision for a practice might include a mission statement that indicates how the practice can relate to the community and what types of patients and medical problems the practice can care for. Your vision should reflect an ideal world in which you have attained success in your practice (and life). Goals in this context mean both short- and long-term ways in which the doctor, practice, and staff can measure their performance.

When your staff is aware of the overall vision you have for your practice and both the short- and long-term goals for yourself and the team, the staff will be more likely to act in ways that are in keeping with this vision.

Suffice it to say that overall vision and goals are important to leadership ability. Do you have a vision and mission statement? Is it articulated in an easy-to-understand manner? Have you shared it with your staff? If so, can your staff understand and recall it?

Key 3: Be a Lifelong Learner

Leaders aren't born; they are made. And they are made just like anything else, through hard work. And that's the price we'll have to pay to achieve that goal, or any goal.
—Vince Lombardi

By this point in your career (and this book), you should be well aware that your education does not and should not cease when you finish your training. In the context of leadership, your ability to recognize and deal with advancements in your profession and profound changes in the way you conduct your practice will have a long-lasting effect on your professional life. If there is one constant that I have observed during the course of my career, it is the rapid pace of change within the medical profession. Our ability to embrace and adapt to changes is directly related to our ability to constantly learn and to teach others.

Continuous learning is a subject that should be embraced wholeheartedly by doctors. In my professional practice, there have been significant changes in our ability to diagnose and treat disorders of the central nervous system, including brain tumors, aneurysms, and a whole host of spinal problems. The adoption of MRI scanning, electronic medical records, and minimally invasive neurosurgical techniques are just a few of the advancements I've seen during the course of my career.

From a business standpoint, we have seen significant changes in how we market the practice, how we deal with referrals, and how our back office systems work. Not only has this required continued learning on my part but also on the part of my staff. As a leader in the practice, it is critical to face these changes enthusiastically, and this does require a certain mindset. The reason I mention it here is this: your staff will naturally resist change, and it will be your job to assist them in embracing and adapting to the changes that will be occurring during the course of your career. As a leader, the success of your practice depends on your ability to manage change.

In the spirit of learning, I would like you to consider the idea of beginning to study examples of leadership that are available in the public eye, both contemporary and historical. Granted, the historical record might not be particularly accurate, but there are many lessons to be learned from consideration of what these people did and how mistakes might be avoided or successes duplicated.

From the political world, Julius Caesar, Louis XIV, and presidents such as George Washington, Thomas Jefferson, and Abraham Lincoln are worth studying for the way they led their people (the good, the bad, and the ugly) and the results they produced. In the military, leaders such as Hannibal, Alexander the Great, Napoleon, and George S. Patton can be examined for their successes and failures. Leaders for social justice, including Mahatma Gandhi, Mother Teresa, and Martin Luther King Jr., should be studied for their approach to the problems they faced. Ask yourself: What was the core problem (or problems) they faced? How did they view this problem and possible solutions? What obstacles did they face in dealing with it? How did they enlist the support of others in their mission?

Business leaders should also be studied. Historical figures like John Rockefeller, Henry Ford, and Andrew Carnegie are worth examining as well as more recent business leaders, including Richard Branson (Virgin Group), Herb Kelleher (Southwest Airlines), and Jeff Bezos (Amazon). What are the fundamental practices that led to their success? How did or how do they treat their employees? What was (or is) it like to work in one of these businesses? Do you agree or disagree with how they work? How did they get their starts? What are their insights on leadership? These are a few of the questions you might consider as you read about them.

I will leave it to you, reader, to consider more contemporary examples of leadership in the political arena and to see the results created from unclear vision and treatment of staff. Pay attention to how crises are dealt with and what accountability (or lack thereof) looks like for major, modern leaders. You may draw your own conclusions on this subject.

Before we move on to how your leadership is expressed to the outside world, I'd like to summarize these first three points. First, having core values and vision to guide you is like having an internal compass and north star to point you in the direction you should follow. You *must* have this if you are to effectively lead others. Second, being open minded and willing to embrace meaningful change is necessary because our culture, and the medical field in particular, is constantly and rapidly evolving. Third, being able to express yourself and your mission is critically important, because you cannot and should not do it all. And the third point is what the next two points are all about.

Now that we have discussed some internal leadership concepts, let's move on to a discussion about external ways in which you can work to get even better at leading your teams.

Key 4: Be a Positive Role Model

The most powerful leadership tool you have
is your own personal example.
—John Wooden

Whether you know it or not, you are setting an example for others with every interaction you have with them. From the way you dress to the way you speak and present yourself to your staff and patients, people are looking to you for cues on how to behave. Now, I'm not perfect and neither are you (probably). It's very difficult to always be on your "A" game, but what I'm saying here is that bringing your conscious awareness into how you are being perceived by those around you is going to help you improve.

When you present yourself in a confident, well-groomed manner, you are sending a message to those around you: "I don't accept poor appearance and behavior, and neither should you." When you are constantly late, you are, in effect, saying, "I am more important than you, and deep down, I don't respect you or your time." In contrast, think about how you feel when you go to meet someone and they are dressed nicely, speak clearly, and are on time for your meeting. I know a surgeon who is constantly late—if he says he'll be there at ten o'clock, you can count on him getting there at eleven. The unspoken message to the staff or patient? "My time is more valuable than yours." He wonders, "Why doesn't the staff respect me?" The answer? The staff thinks, "You have no respect for me, so why should I respect you?"

As a role model and leader in your practice, you have the ability to decide whether to emulate this type of behavior. The point is this: if you accept tardiness, poor grooming, and sloppy speech in yourself, those around you will consider it acceptable in themselves, and their behavior will follow. This is important, and we will delve into this more deeply in a future chapter when we discuss marketing. For now, consider this: you are asking your patients to trust you with their lives. For them to trust you, they must respect you, and for that to happen, they need to know you respect them. When you were a student or resident, it really didn't matter much how you looked or acted—you were just a student. However, when you assume the role of the attending physician, the trusted adviser, you must play the part. This means dressing and acting like someone who can be trusted with one's life.

How you act and react to the inevitable changes in your practice will be reflected by your staff—if you are impolite and condescending in your interactions with patients, insurance company employees, or peer-reviewing physicians, your staff will see this and consider it acceptable. They will mirror your behavior in their own interactions.

Recently, I came across a post on social media by a friend of mine. She said, "I have had it with Dr. X's office—they are so rude, and I am looking for another doctor to care for me and my family. Does anyone have any suggestions?" I don't know what event prompted this response, but I think it's likely that such behavior was probably considered acceptable by the supervising physician in that office.

In my experience, poor treatment of staff by the doctor or manager inevitably leads to poor treatment of the patients or clients. Richard Branson, founder of Virgin Group, says, "Clients do not come first; employees come first—so if you take good care of your employees, they will take good care of your clients." He also said, "Train people well enough so that they can leave, but treat them well enough that they won't want to."

Here are some behavioral considerations for you to review and think about:

1. Demonstrate confidence in your decision-making and actions. You have likely overcome adversity along your path to becoming a physician. When faced with difficult decisions, say to yourself: "I've faced difficulties before and made it through. I will make it through this one as well." Hold your head up and carry on. Your staff and others will see this and be inspired.

2. Be yourself. Everyone has a unique persona; some are boisterous and extroverted, while others are calm and quiet. Let your own personality come through in your interactions. Forced behavioral patterns will be obvious to those around you, and it will appear you are faking it. People will question whether you are faking other things.

3. Show respect for others. Over the years, I've seen really reprehensible behavior from doctors in the way they treat others who are not in positions of authority. While this type of behavior might give the person some pleasure, in the long run it is very self-destructive. These days, there are so

many people involved in the care of our patients, and even a small amount of disrespect to anyone can lead to negative comments made to the patient, which may be detrimental to care. Here is a (probably incomplete) list of the people involved in scheduling and completing an operation:

- The office staff schedules a patient—let's call her Sally—for a visit, and while in the office, the patient interacts with the receptionist, medical assistant, scheduler, and insurance specialist.

- After arriving at the hospital, Sally will see people in the admitting office, nurses and medical assistants on the floor, and transporters. She'll be directed to anesthesiologists and anesthetists as well as nurses and scrub techs in surgery.

- Postoperatively, there will be people in the postanesthesia care unit as well as discharge specialists.

This patient could easily interact with fifty people along the way, all of whom play a significant role in the care of this person. Every one of these people is an individual who has the same wants and needs as you do: they want to feel needed, and more importantly, appreciated for the effort they put forth.

Here is your challenge: Find someone who takes great care to be an exemplary employee, and go out of your way to thank them for the work they do. Do this regularly (weekly or even daily), and see how the attitude and respect they have for you and others improves.

Raise your personal expectations for your own behavior. Find a role model in your personal or public life, or even a historical figure, to emulate. In this manner, you can work on improving yourself on a regular basis. As a result, you might find yourself to be a role model to those around you, as they observe you taking active steps to better yourself.

Key 5: Connect

Alone we can do so little; together we can do so much.
—Helen Keller

No doctor can do everything alone. That means we must inspire others to work for and with us to achieve anything. And that means having an effective connection between you and your team. Here are six (simple) ways to better connect:

1. Focus. In our hyperconnected world, it's very easy to become distracted. As physicians, we have so many ways in which our attention can be diverted that it's very easy to lose focus. There is also the myth that multitasking is a good thing. When speaking to others (staff and patients), give them your full attention—it will help to prevent misunderstandings and assumptions on your part.

2. Have empathy. As physicians, we all have (hopefully) developed some degree of empathy for others along the way, especially when interacting with patients and their families. With respect to communicating with others in your leadership role, it's sometimes easy to forget how important empathy for their circumstances can help you in your communication. There is a quote I like (attributed to several people): "I may forget what you said or did, but I will never forget how you made me feel." It's true—people will remember insults or put-downs for years, even decades. So try to put yourself in others' shoes when speaking to them.

3. Listen. I like to say we have two ears and only one mouth for a reason: we need to listen twice as much as we talk. Try to listen actively to others, and by that I mean hearing the words and also the emotional context behind the words. Interpreting body language can also be helpful here if you are speaking in person, as people will frequently make gestures and position themselves in ways that are at odds with the words they are speaking. Like Andy Stanley once said, "Leaders who don't listen will eventually be surrounded by people who have nothing to say."

4. Be clear. We've all been the unfortunate audience to speakers who drone on and on about things in an unclear manner. Use simple and straightforward words and sentences. People will be much less likely to misinterpret what you are saying. Be brief and to the point. When and if questions are raised, expand as necessary.

5. Offer praise. As a resident, I once (OK, more than once) made a surgical error. My attending surgeon stopped and said (to the medical students in the room): "Did you see the stupid thing that Dr. Corradino just did?" (I'm remembering this thirty years later.) That insult really hurt! Offer praise in public but criticism (even if it's helpful) in private. We like to be recognized for our contributions in front of others, but if there is one thing that everyone hates, it's to be criticized in public. Unless it's absolutely necessary, leave your critical discussions for times when you are not in a public setting—and when criticism is necessary, begin in a friendly, helpful way.

6. Thank people. Finally, show appreciation for others whenever appropriate. Thank them for their help in getting a job done well or whenever someone has gone the extra mile for you.

* * *

Rather than looking in the mirror and accepting how you are, take action to improve yourself in these areas of your life. As a (reformed) introvert, I can tell you that things are much more enjoyable if you spend time learning to better connect with others. Take the time to think about yourself, your values, and what makes you tick. Doing so improves your decision-making and helps you navigate through your day. Be present when you are with others, and strive to understand them before you make your own points. Many of these skills are simple to understand but deceptively hard to act on regularly. If you actively work on improving yourself in these areas of your life, your ability to positively influence those around you will increase immensely.

I will leave you with this quote: "Leaders are the creators of their lives. Followers let life happen to them."

Be the leader you were meant to become!

ACTION STEPS

1. Be a lifelong learner: Read about a historical leader today, and see what you can glean from their example.

2. Connect with someone: Thank a member of staff who's gone the extra mile for you.

3. Who's your role model? Think about someone who's played a part in shaping you. Write down three characteristics of that person that stand out the most, and try to emulate that person in those ways going forward.

CHAPTER 8

FOUNDATION FOUR

Working with Winners

You're the sum total of the five people that
you hang around with the most.
—Jim Rohn

You may not realize it, but you're subjected to the thoughts and influences of other people, including your peers, staff, family, and friends. The more you listen to and become influenced by these other people, the more they will affect you in many ways: how you view the world, how you interact with others, your disposition, and even how you progress in your career.

So who are these influencers? That's exactly what this chapter will discuss.

CAREFUL CURATION

Enact very careful curation when choosing your circle of influencers. The people who you, as a physician, must be aware of include the following:

CIRCLE OF INFLUENCERS:

- Staff
- Associates
- Doctors in the doctors' lounge
- Individuals in professional organizations

Staff

First of all, these influencers are your staff. Young doctors who are joining a practice probably have little control over which staff members are assigned to them. Let your staff know your expectations about how they are to act, and hold them accountable. (I understand this may be difficult as "the new face in town," but if you are in the right practice, your associates should understand and back you up.) This may be necessary to bring them over to your way of thinking. Your staff will look to you for cues about how to act and what is acceptable and unacceptable behavior toward each other and toward your patients. Your leadership and management abilities can be useful in this setting when it is necessary to mold your staff into performing to your expectations.

As you move along in your career, you may have more influence in hiring employees who have a growth attitude, who smile, who are happy to see you, and who listen when you teach them and help them become better at their jobs. This is very important so that when you arrive in your office, you're not faced with people who clearly don't want to be there. Like it or not, that will have an effect on your attitude and decrease your effectiveness. When you hire someone, you need to spend the time to train them properly. Then you need to counsel them if they don't achieve the levels of performance that you want. If they don't do it, then you need to terminate them.

As an example, we once had an employee, Sally, who was the receptionist in our office. She was very competent at what she did, but she was single minded in her job, and there was no variation in what she did on a daily basis. When something would come in that was not quite what she expected, she became very negative and almost chided patients for their lack of planning or resources, and so forth. Over time, she turned off a lot of patients, and we didn't really realize it until she quit. When she quit, the first thing that happened was many patients said, "I'm so glad you got rid of your receptionist, because I just dreaded coming in here and having to deal with her."

That's clearly not the kind of person you want to have to see every day. Can she be trained to see how her actions have an effect on everyone in the practice and to improve? If she can, great, but if not, you need the managerial skills to let her move on.

How do you know if you have one of those people? You can send a mystery shopper in to call the office or come to the office with questions and just see what kind of response this person gives to them. If they give them a bad response, then you know you need to address that. Unfortunately, there are staff members who are resistant to change, and their behavior is inconsistent with the practice mission and ideals, and they need to be shown the door. This is likely to happen, I hate to say, so you need to be able to establish a process for this as well.

Associates

Next, you need to consider others who you associate with, including other physicians and midlevel providers in your practice. If you join a practice in which there's a lot of negativity about finances and regulations, trouble dealing with hospital administration, and so forth, you're going to become negative as well. Parenthetically, if you've spent the time to identify your values, mission, and ideal practice setting, you will likely have avoided joining this practice to begin with. (I'm going to assume that the value of "negativity" is not something you aspire to.)

I was once in a practice with another physician who only had negative things to say. No matter what the situation was, he looked for the negativity in it, and eventually, I couldn't stand working with this fellow anymore, and I had to ask him to leave the practice because I recognized what this association was doing to me. Was it difficult? It certainly was. Was it worth it? Absolutely.

Doctors' Lounge

Another place where negativity happens is in the doctors' lounge. When you go to the doctors' lounge, you tend to see a lot of doctors who are looking for somebody to talk with about whatever ills they're dealing with. Over the course of my career, we've had things like the Y2K scare and significant changes in the CPT coding. We've had the establishment of the Affordable Care Act. We've had the change to the ICD-10 coding. All of these things were looked at as potentially disrupting practice finances, and adjustments were necessary.

Dealing with them involved finding out what the problem was and establishing a plan to fix it. If you hang around with the kind of people who simply have negative things to say about an issue and don't really offer a plan for fixing it, it can turn you into a sullen person as well. People can be problem focused or solution focused. Which are you? If you associate only with problem-focused people, you will tend to look at things negatively. If you focus on solutions, you will find yourself looking for ways to solve problems.

Professional Organizations

The same principle applies for your professional organizations. You have local and regional organizations, and these are frequently composed of people who simply want a forum in which to complain about things. It's likely you have to be involved in some of these groups, and in many cases, you won't really have much choice, but limiting your exposure to them is probably a wise thing.

So in summary, you have your staff, your associates, and your organizations that will have an active influence on your attitude. It goes without saying that your family, friends, and associates outside of work will also affect your outlook. My advice: become single minded in associating as much as possible with positive influencers both personally and professionally. Keep as far as possible from those who might have a negative influence on you or your career. There's too much at stake for you to spend any more time than necessary with those people who will keep you from performing at your best.

> MY ADVICE: BECOME SINGLE MINDED IN ASSOCIATING AS MUCH AS POSSIBLE WITH POSITIVE INFLUENCERS BOTH PERSONALLY AND PROFESSIONALLY.

DEVELOP YOUR OWN CIRCLE OF INFLUENCE

We all need advisers, professionals who you can turn to for counsel when the time arises. Why do doctors need them, and when should we start to look for them? Because of the unique nature of a career in medicine, we have specialized needs in many areas of life. Most doctors have little knowledge about medical or malpractice law, about the tax code and financial planning, so we need specialists in many of these areas. What follows are my opinions about building a quality group of advisers as we go through our careers.

These advisers include the following:

- Legal advisers

- Financial advisers

- Investment advisers

- Insurance agents

- Mentors

- Mastermind groups

Legal Advisers

Physicians need both personal and professional legal advisers, because we're essentially tiptoeing through a minefield fraught with threats to our well-being and livelihood throughout our careers. As we are aware, when something goes wrong, the general society immediately looks for someone to blame, whether it's a delivery person slipping on your porch and breaking an ankle or a patient suffering a bad reaction to a drug you prescribed. When these things happen, you'll need a smart and knowledgeable legal team to advise you. It's probably a good idea to establish a relationship with at least one or two attorneys early in your career.

In addition, you might need legal advice to establish your estate plan and advice about how to set up trusts or other entities to hold assets such as educational funds. From experience, I can tell you that having a friend or even a casual acquaintance you can call when trouble arises means a lot in terms of your peace of mind. Early in my career, I had a patient who threatened to sue me for a relatively minor and known complication of a very straightforward surgery. In addition to the lawyer who was assigned my case by the malpractice carrier, I called an attorney friend who gave me much useful advice and helped me with some of the emotional turmoil associated with the threat.

Financial Advisers

Rather than just one or two, there should be several independent advisers you can trust. Tax planning and budgeting concerns should be addressed by a CPA who can advise on how to legally reduce your tax liability and create a workable budget. Next, a financial planner can help you create an overall strategy for savings, budgeting, investing, and planning for educational costs and retirement. Financial planners can be commission based (not advisable, due to inherent conflicts of interest in their advice) or fee only.

I once had my money with a commission-based adviser who frequently had me buying and selling securities (in retrospect, I found that he was buying at the historical highs and selling at the lows). After a while, I began to have the impression that he was "churning the account" for his commissions. I have since learned that this is how many of the big brokerage houses work their accounts, so maybe it was not all his fault. In contrast, fee-only planners will help you create a financial plan and revisit it on a regular basis. There are certified and chartered planners. You should familiarize yourself with the various entities and understand how they are compensated.

Investment Advisers

Investment advisers help you establish where you're going to put your money and see if it's reaching the benchmarks that you set along the way. Unlike financial planners, they generally do not help you develop a full-fledged financial plan. Typically, they will recommend an asset-allocation plan for your investments based on your age, financial goals, income, and risk tolerance.

For example, if you are young and able to withstand risk to your portfolio, your adviser might have you put more money into riskier stocks, such as stock in an unproven company. If you are closer to retirement and can't afford to take a big hit to your account, your adviser might allocate a larger percentage of your account into "safer" investment products, such as high-quality, tax-free municipal bonds. In any case, no matter what choice you make, I highly recommend you invest in your financial education by reading up on the subject. The *Wall Street Journal* and *Fortune* magazine have excellent advice on improving your financial education, and there are a wide number of books on the subject. The Teaching Company (thegreatcourses.com) also has an excellent course on financial literacy.

Insurance Agents

You also need to consider protecting your assets and dealing with loss, should that occur. An insurance agent can help you in planning your life, disability, and property insurance needs.

Insurance agents can be independent or associated with larger companies or conglomerates. If associated with a conglomerate, it is likely an agent will be steering you toward a certain company's products. Try to get an independent opinion to assess how much and what types of insurance you will need.

Mentors

The concept of having such a coach or a mentor as an adviser has lately been gaining popularity, and I can personally attest to the value. This person can be another doctor, or even a nonphysician, who is further along in their career and can help you with the pitfalls that you're likely to see at certain stages of your career. They might be a senior professor from your training program who you can turn to for advice along the way, a paid coach, or even a senior member of your group.

A mentor or coach can bring perspective and experience—they can help you define long-term goals and hold you accountable as you move toward them. They can serve as trusted advisers for your discussed issues, and they can help you expand your network and introduce you to others who might help you advance your career. Ultimately, the goal of working with a mentor or coach is to inspire you to reach new heights.

Early on in my postresidency career, there were several physicians whom I called on a regular basis to ask about problems that I had never seen before (even after seven years of training!), so I learned the value in having a mentor early on in my career. A good friend of mine joined a large group practice right out of training, and senior members of his group guided him along for a period until he developed enough experience and self-confidence. Throughout my career, I have frequently sought the advice of those more senior than I and been grateful for their guidance. Some of the specialty societies now sponsor mentorship programs, and I highly recommend you consider signing on for a mentor.

Mastermind Groups

A mastermind group is a group of people who come together with the intention of helping each other achieve goals. More than simply a group meeting, a mastermind combines brainstorming, accountability, and support. The concept was first popularized by the author Napoleon Hill in his classic book, *Think and Grow Rich*. He studied the habits of some of the most successful businessmen of the early twentieth century and attributed much of their success to being members of various mastermind alliances. Hill described a mastermind as "the coordination of knowledge and effort of two or more people who work toward a definite purpose" and noted that "no two minds ever come together without thereby creating a third, invisible, intangible force, which may be likened to a third mind (the mastermind)."

A business mastermind would focus on problems and solutions, such as growth, operations, customer service and retention, and product or service development. In contrast, a physician mastermind's focus might be medical issues within your specialty or common problems faced by all physicians.

Mastermind groups exist in person and on the internet, where other like-minded individuals and entrepreneurs talk about how they might approach and deal with obstacles that are personal or work related, or you can establish your own mastermind group in your community. The concept has been around for many years, probably even before Napoleon Hill coined the term.

Personally, for many years, I've been a member of a large mastermind group for entrepreneurs, including financial planners, attorneys, and businesspeople. We get together four times a year and talk about issues common to entrepreneurs. I have found that this is very helpful to me in how I look at the business aspects of my practice. I think that aspect of a mastermind group and being part of a community where you have like-minded individuals who are facing the same sorts of problems is invaluable, because you recognize that you're not alone in dealing with similar concerns in every industry.

* * *

In summary, building a powerful support network of like-minded individuals will have a tremendous, positive effect on your career. It is the fourth of the five cornerstones of a solid foundation for your practice. We will address the final one, building your practice, in the next, and final, chapter.

ACTION STEPS

1. Begin to systematically examine all your relationships.

2. Resolve to spend less time with people who drain your energy.

3. Seek out individuals who empower you to rise to greater heights personally and professionally.

4. Remember that this is an active process and should continue throughout your career.

CHAPTER 9

FOUNDATION FIVE

Building Your Practice

The best marketing strategy ever: care.
—Gary Vaynerchuk

P ractice building is an integral part of your professional life and the final foundation that we'll discuss here as we conclude the book. When it comes to practice building, do not leave this to underlings—growing your ideal practice is too important to your professional satisfaction. In this chapter, we'll discuss steps, like building trust in the community, that should be taken into consideration as you begin to build your ideal practice.

HOW TO BUILD YOUR IDEAL PRACTICE

As I mentioned earlier, following my residency I took a position as the only neurosurgeon in a small community hospital not far from a large city (Philadelphia). This was a job with an income guarantee for two years; at first, it seemed like an ideal position. When I arrived, the hospital marketing "department" took me around to various primary care offices to meet and greet the referral sources they anticipated would be sending me patients. We all stood around awkwardly talking about my training and experience in caring for patients with various neurosurgical problems, until I left and they could get back to caring for their patients.

I returned to my office (with my staff of two) and read books while I waited for doctors' offices to call and make appointments or for the hospital ER to call with a consult. As you might imagine, this was not a formula for success. Although I liked the community, I felt very uninspired and even bored. I needed to work, to be in surgery, and to use the skills I had trained so long and hard to acquire. Soon I found myself looking for another position and ended up in Tennessee, where I joined a busy practice in a small community.

There I was immediately engaged in doing a wide range of surgery, including spine, brain tumors, and aneurysms. This was what I had anticipated when I finished my residency, yet things were not always rosy. Patients did not seem to relish coming to see me, and I frequently found it difficult to convince them of my proposed treatment plan. Sometimes I recommended surgery, and they sought a second opinion from my partner or even left the practice. Many times, I recommended nonsurgical treatments, and they seemed to be disappointed they were not going to have surgery! What was going on here?

Well, as you might imagine, in both settings there was no real plan to build or grow my practice. All parties had made the *Field of Dreams* assumption so common in the medical community: "If you build it, they will come." In my case, I thought, "I went to medical school at the University of Virginia and trained in Boston and at the University of Maryland—that should be enough for patients to believe and trust me." While that might have worked fifty years ago, it is not a formula for success now.

Because of mass media, the internet, and social media, patients are much more able to research their problems and seek their own solutions. They do not rely entirely on direction from medical professionals to point them to a certain practitioner for care. This fragmentation creates an opportunity for the forward-thinking physician to establish their own ideal practice by developing and implementing a plan.

In this chapter, we will discuss the concepts behind that plan and outline it. In the past, it was said that all you needed to succeed was affability, availability, and ability. While all of that is true, if your patients don't know it, it's not going to help you build your practice.

Steps to consider when building your practice, which this chapter covers, include the following:

STEPS TO BUILDING YOUR PRACTICE:

- Identify your ideal patient

- Establish trust

- Build a community presence

- Collect testimonials

- Have a well-trained, communicative staff

- Invest in social media marketing

IDENTIFY YOUR IDEAL PATIENT

The first step in this process is understanding what kind of patient you want to care for, the avatar of your ideal patient. Rather than taking any problem that walks through the door, focus on your specialty, what you truly love to do.

For a gastroenterologist, that might be someone who has a gastric ulcer. That's their main thing. They love gastric ulcers. They love to do endoscopies on them. They love to treat them and to see whether the treatments are working and so forth. For me, it's a patient with a problem best treated by neurosurgery—it could be a certain type of brain tumor or a herniated cervical disc. The patient may or may not need surgery, but they do need my expertise in recommending a treatment plan.

The first step in establishing the kind of practice that you want to grow is knowing who that patient is. Understand that this is not going to happen overnight. You're not going to move to Richmond or Kansas City this month and find yourself busy with your ideal patients two months from now. This is a long-term project, but it will be incredibly rewarding because when you've established this plan, you will find yourself doing things you've trained for and that you enjoy.

ESTABLISH TRUST

Patients need to trust you. This was one of the missing links in the early days of my practice. Patients needed to know that I was for real. I came to the community with degrees and accolades, but no one had ever heard of me or seen me. I was a name on a door with a piece of paper on the wall.

How else do you establish trust? Patients want to know that they can believe you and understand you. They need to know you are a safe choice and available to care for them—you have to earn their trust. From a sharp website and a constant, dependable online presence to a newspaper column, there are ways to document your expertise and earn trust.

> THEY NEED TO KNOW YOU ARE A SAFE CHOICE AND AVAILABLE TO CARE FOR THEM— YOU HAVE TO EARN THEIR TRUST.

The following written items will help you establish trust:

1. A sharp website. Hire a designer to get you set up with a good-looking, user-friendly website, or at least let a professional have a look at your current site and offer advice on how to update it.

2. A regularly updated blog. Ideally, the topics presented will speak to your ideal patient. In the case of an expert in diabetes, some examples might be, "How exercise can help control

your sugars," or "What to avoid over the holidays to keep you feeling strong." This establishes your expertise in the field.

3. A Facebook page. A social media presence can link to your blog and website, keeping you in the minds of your patients. But a post must be done regularly, several times a week preferably, if it's going to be worthwhile. More on social media in a bit.

4. Brochures. A brochure or pamphlet describing your practice philosophy or how you deal with the main problems seen in your practice (or your "ideal problem"). If the brochures have your name on them or the practice's name on them, it's going to lend a lot more credibility than if it's a generic thing that's written by some nameless person. A brochure on your area of expertise—something informational, like nonsurgical treatments for back pain or migraines—would be beneficial as a tangible item people can hold on to.

5. Media. Whether it's a newspaper or a magazine, media is great for building a practice. Any time an article is written about you, it will enhance your credibility to have reprints framed around the office or printed and available for your patients. Consider sending out press releases on technology advancements available at your practice or human-interest stories from your own happy patients that could tug at the heartstrings.

6. A column. I used to write a quarterly newspaper article, a health Q&A, for the local newspaper. We called it "Healthy Advice," and that had a huge effect on patients. Patients would come into the office and say, "Oh, I read your article and it meant so much. It was so good." And I was kind of blown away by it, because the Q&As were very short and

really basic, but that kind of thing did a huge thing for my practice, and it was fairly easy. So if that opportunity exists for doctors, I would say jump on it because it really will build your reputation very quickly.

7. A newsletter. A newsletter can be very helpful in keeping you and your practice in the minds of your patients—newsletter content and production is a subject that entire books have been written on. Budding practices would greatly benefit from sending out an e-newsletter to everyone, from patients to referring physicians.

8. A book. Finally, a book on your ideal subject, that you have either written or contributed to, would be a huge addition to your ability to build trust in your patient base. If someone is going to consider you versus the doctor down the street, they're going to go to you because you wrote the book.

BUILD A COMMUNITY PRESENCE

The next thing is whether you have any presence in your community, and that can include joining community organizations like the chamber of commerce or the rotary club, for example, or regularly doing community service by, say, leading a class one evening every few months. You can use these classes to address a specific problem that you take care of. For example, arthritis in the knee might be a popular problem that members of your community may be interested in learning how to deal with and that you can help them with. If you are a rheumatologist or orthopedic surgeon, you would then be known as the local expert on this subject, and you could build on that.

The goal is to become known in the community, meet more people who aren't necessarily in medicine. Personally, I've been involved with Toastmasters for several years now, and it does help. It gives me a presence. For a while I also ran a small group on high performance in the community that was part of Meetup.com. The relationships I formed there led to people who ended up needing surgery from me. They weren't necessarily part of the group, but people who were would refer their friends to me.

All these little things add up. It's not going to be one big thing that all of a sudden is going to turn you into the world's greatest and most popular person. But little by little by little, and over a period of time, you create a brand and a persona in your community.

The hospital I work with does community outreach, and it has a presence in the local mall here. It's asked me to give talks there, which I've done multiple times. I think that's a great way to establish yourself in the community as an expert. Again, it's all a big process, and it's not something that is going to change everything for you overnight. You're not going to all of a sudden become the go-to expert in one day. But over a period of months or years, you truly will become a recognized expert in whatever area of expertise, if you purposely make an effort to do so. That's what this is all about.

At one point we hired a brand consultant, and to me, it was very unsatisfying and extremely expensive. It was thousands of dollars. It ended up not being worth it, because when I think about it, more than just having a nice and consistent-looking logo, you really have to build your reputation in your community on good work over long periods of time. On the other hand, finding a professional who can help you build an organic audience with a marketing campaign of substance would be worth your while.

No matter what you do, you cannot manufacture this type of positive brand for yourself or your practice. You can't suddenly produce a billboard and then have people running to see you. That's not how it works with being a doctor and building up a good practice. You have to think about it in a purposeful, long-term, organic way.

Collect Testimonials

If you have either written or video testimonials that you can promote at your office or website, those will also lend credibility to you as an authority in your subject. Testimonials that are video testimonials with real people rather than actors can be excellent for establishing that type of credibility.

There are many ways in which testimonials can be used. Whether it's written online or done via video, what you want to do is create an overwhelming preponderance of evidence that you are the expert in the field, that you're a good person to go to with X, Y, or Z problems. So when people come in the door, they're preprogrammed to know that you're good at what you do, you're an expert, and you're the right person to help them.

Because isn't that what you want as a physician? You want people to look at you as the expert. You want people to believe what you tell them. You want people to be assured that you can help them get better. The more that you can do, the more of these things that you can stack on top of each other, the easier it will be to make that mental leap for the patient.

A good many years ago, the hospital I worked with actively sought out former patients in order to get testimonials and try to build up a marketing campaign around neurosurgery. The testimonials were printed onto a spread, along with the patient's photograph, which was framed for our offices. That way when you come into the room, patients are already happy to see you. You're an expert; you're a celebrity. You've got a whole spread written about you, and you look like you know what you're doing. So it becomes a lot easier for them to take your advice and do what you tell them to do to help get them better.

Have a Well-Trained, Communicative Staff

Having your staff members buy into building your practice, and their role in it, is important as well. It's really critical that you train your staff and treat them well because they're the face of your practice. They're probably going to have more interaction with patients than you are between setting up appointments with patients, greeting them when they come in, getting taken to their exam room, and having a nurse or medical assistant take their blood.

All those little things can make a difference to people. I've known of practices where staff truly didn't know what the doctor was trained to do. They didn't know what procedures the doctor could or couldn't do. Those workers can make or break your ability to bring in new patients. When they can say things like, "Well, Dr. Jones's area of expertise is hypertension in elderly women," that establishes you as the expert in the patients' mind and sets you up for success. That person will tell their friend or tennis partner, and before you know it, you'll be the community's expert on elderly women with hypertension.

If you're a new doctor, it's important to meet with the staff to explain both your specialties as well as how you expect them to treat your patients. That small step at the beginning can save you a lot of time and headaches later dealing with unhappy or frustrated patients.

Invest in Social Media Marketing

Social media is an opportunity for physicians to become education leaders in the community; however, many of us need some help in that department. In search of some expertise, I reached out to Amy

Cathey, marketing professor and executive director of graduate and executive programs for the Haslam College of Business at the University of Tennessee, Knoxville. She explained several reasons why it's so crucial, particularly in this digital age, for physicians to get on board with platforms like Facebook that can further our reach.

First, the integration of social media into our daily lives makes the platform such an important construct to understand in spaces like healthcare. Cathey says, "Especially with patients, social media is an important way that people receive information, and they look at healthcare-related information over social media as a very credible source."

According to Cathey, social media is a not-to-be-missed opportunity for physicians, or else we yield that space to third-party providers, like WebMD. Meanwhile, you could be providing a valuable, credible resource for the community, further establishing trust and building your practice.

Second, educating patients through social media, be it through a link to your company blog or a snippet of useful advice in a post, saves you time. Patients can walk in the office already educated with the information the doctor would want them to have. Cathey says, "It makes it more efficient [and] ensures a better fit before the patient ever walks in the door, that the physician's perspective and point of view is similar to what the patient feels like is going to be appropriate for them."

Furthermore, she says, to miss the social media train now means falling behind instead of staying current and building your brand on what is an increasingly effective medium. In 2019, the Pew Research Center did a study[3] that says that 69 percent of US adults use at least

---

3   Pew Research Center, "Social Media Fact Sheet," June 12, 2019, https://www. pewresearch.org/internet/fact-sheet/social-media/.

one social media site—that's basically seven out of every ten adults. Compare that to 20 percent ten years ago, and it's clear that in five years, even more Americans will have at least some access to social media.

So how can a physician get up to speed now? Cathey says that you must be prepared to invest in maintaining your process over time. A social media professional can do that, taking care to not only manage your social channels but also keep your overall digital presence alive and well with continued website updates.

"If you can't post on Facebook once a week or even once a month, then don't have a Facebook page," Cathey says. The best practice would be to post at least an update once a week, if not multiple times a week. If you can't create a structure where you can get something up even once a month, it says more negative than positive things about your abilities. With online tools like Hootsuite available, a smaller practice can schedule posts in advance, scheduling in one day or week enough posts to sustain a presence through a longer period of time. "So you don't have to outsource it," she says. "It is possible to do what you need to do internally."

In the end, what you want to do is use your social media platform as an outlet to educate. One way to do that is, as mentioned before, through patient testimonials, which are often posted on social media. These reviews can be educational and so much more effective than your typical product review. "These are people whose lives have been changed by a particular treatment, or surgery, or whatever the case may be," Cathey says. "And they're more than happy to share their experience as a testimonial or as a way of educating others."

Being able to use that in social media is a really powerful way to engage those patients, and future ones too.

* * *

In conclusion, all of this can be done in a very measured manner, establishing you early on in your career. Otherwise, it's just haphazard and whoever comes your way, comes your way. I know a doctor in my community who regularly complains that he just doesn't see the kind of patients that he wants to see. How do they know that he's the expert on certain subjects other than him telling them directly? He doesn't have an online presence. He doesn't give lectures. He's not on TV. He doesn't write an article in the newspaper. He just expects it to happen. That's simply not the way our interconnected world works.

Working with a marketing person, either in your practice or in the hospital in your community, from day one will soon enable you to be seen as the go-to person for the problems you're trained to treat.

ACTION STEPS

1. Begin to think about your ideal patient now.

2. Build a virtual marketing structure to direct at your ideal patient.

3. Reap the benefits of your deliberate actions!

CONCLUSION

The best time to plant a tree was twenty years
ago; the second best time is now.
—Chinese proverb

n conclusion, these are the five cornerstones that, in my experience, lay the foundation for a highly successful career in medicine:

- Planning: taking the time to work out a strategic plan for yourself and your practice, the first cornerstone for your personal and professional success

- Values: establishing your values

- Communication: cultivating your communication skills to work effectively with others

- Working with winners: developing a powerful team around you

- Building your practice: working actively to build your practice from day one, with effective and inexpensive marketing techniques

It takes so much more than simply attending a good school or training program to prepare you for a lifetime of making the best decisions you can possibly make for your business. I hope that this book can be a turning point for you, just as discovering (the hard way) that I'd hired an unreliable accountant all those years ago in Kingsport, Tennessee, was a turning point for me. If only I'd known then what I know now. That's why I wrote this book—so that you can establish your values and direction now, before learning some hard lessons of your own in the future.

From pinpointing and leading with your personal and professional values to using compassionate communication with staff and patients to surrounding yourself with an A-plus team from the start, these key foundations will form the basis for your career success and help you go home from your satisfying job with a smile on your face.

Remember, education is a lifelong responsibility. Working with this in mind, you will find professional and personal satisfaction with your career. To your success!

CPSIA information can be obtained
at www.ICGtesting.com
Printed in the USA
BVHW090940081220
595176BV00016B/326

9 781642 251449